CREATING YOUR
GARDEN FARM

How to grow fruit and vegetables and raise chickens and bees

NICKI TRENCH

CICO BOOKS
LONDON NEW YORK

First published in 2010 by CICO Books
This edition published in 2013 by CICO Books
an imprint of Ryland Peters & Small Ltd
20–21 Jockey's Fields, London WC1R 4BW

www.cicobooks.com

10 9 8 7 6 5 4 3 2 1

A CIP catalogue record for this book is available
from the British Library.

ISBN: 978 1 908862 84 6

Printed in China

Project editor: Gillian Haslam
Text editor: Jo Richardson
Designer: Christine Wood
Photographer: David Merewether
(photographs on page 71, 75, 76, 79, 87, 108,
111 and 133, step 6 by Caroline Hughes)
Illustrator: Michael Hill

For digital editions, visit
www.cicobooks.com/apps.php

CONTENTS

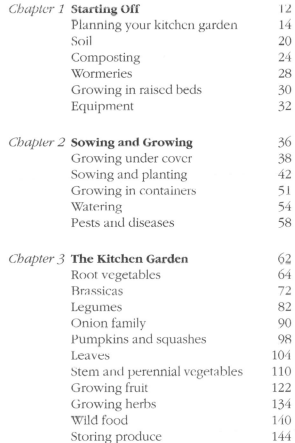

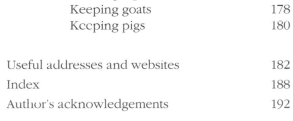

Introduction

The enthusiasm for growing your own produce and cooking fresh and local extends much further than simply reducing costs. People are feeling tricked; we no longer recognize the true shapes, colours and textures of the plastic-wrapped and over-packaged produce that appears on the shelves of our supermarkets. We're presented with a world removed from reality. Headless, footless and fatless chickens encased in cellophane; apples, carrots and tomatoes all uniform in shape and colour; broccoli trimmed and wrapped so perfectly that no one knows what the real plant looks like. When you grow your own produce, you see the plant for how it is – the beautiful deep-red veins that run through beetroot leaves, strangely shaped carrots unlike the straight, uniform specimens you see in the shops, or the majestic thistle-like flower of the artichoke.

OPPOSITE: Ripe, crunchy apples waiting to be picked and eaten straight from the tree.

BELOW: Fresh eggs with bright yellow yolks laid daily from your own hens.

Embracing the oddball

People now reject odd-shaped vegetables because they probably think they're from outer space. With all this perfection around in the kitchen, maybe we apply the same weird standards to people, rejecting the apparently odd from our lives. The world of advertising has a lot to answer for. And how many children can name the various vegetables when they see them, let alone recognize the plant, or know where cuts of meat come from?

Making a change for the better

With the growing awareness of the impact that food miles has on the environment and the advantages of eating non-sprayed, local and organic food, people are once more opting to grow their own. In the UK, the sales of vegetable seeds have now overtaken those of flowers and hen husbandry is outstripping the keeping of rabbits and guinea pigs as pets. Of course, this all makes sense. Domestic pets have their uses: cats are great mouse and rat catchers, and dogs will keep unwelcome cats off the fresh soil in your vegetable patch. But nothing is as good and tasty as a bright yellow egg produced by your own free-range, happy hens.

Using your time and space wisely

The space you have will determine just how far you go in being a garden farmer. If you have a small patio, with room for only a few pots, this shouldn't put you off. You can grow a wide variety of vegetables and fruits in a small space and many varieties will enthusiastically grow wonderful produce. If you have a larger space, plan carefully and you'll be able to have enough beds to rotate your crops, helping to maintain their health and that of the soil, as well

as the opportunity to keep hens, bees or even goats and pigs. And that means you'll be well on the way to being self-sufficient.

Animals will need time devoted to them, and they also need to be kept in an appropriate area that is best for them and best for you. I once kept a goat and decided to let it have free run of the garden, until it ate through my internet cable. It has to work both ways: an escaped pig may be fun to watch being chased back to its pen by amused bystanders, but it can totally destroy your vegetables in two minutes flat.

In our modern society, time is an issue. Most people simply cannot devote their whole time to becoming totally self-sufficient, but even if you make just a small impact on your own and your family's lives, you will be contributing to the good of the environment and your and their well-being. There may be times of the year when your home-grown produce will be sparse, but with a little planning, you should be able to grow at least something for the kitchen table in every season.

Benefiting your health

Spending time in your garden has enormous health benefits. Not only will you be working outside in the fresh air, but digging and preparing your soil, weeding and turning over your compost will render visits to the gym unnecessary. Who wants to waste time on a treadmill when you could be working towards growing and producing your own food instead? Many local communities are setting up community allotments where they're finding that working with the soil, besides offering enormous physical health benefits, gives people a sense of purpose and brings well-being to their minds.

Vegetables are best picked fresh, as they contain natural sugars that quickly turn to starch. Commercially grown vegetables have often lost the majority of their goodness by the time they reach the supermarket shelves and, what's more, have lost half their flavour. As soon as you start to harvest and eat your own produce, you'll be bowled over by the explosion of flavours that makes shop-bought produce fade into insignificance.

Overcoming the age barrier

It doesn't matter at what stage you're at in life when contemplating a garden farm. Vegetables, fruits, herbs and animals will not care how old or young you are and they will do their best to work with you. If you have children, try to involve them as much as you can in choosing and growing your produce and in looking after the animals. This will teach them how to cultivate the food that they will eat as well as a sense of commitment and nurture when keeping animals.

I'm often taken by surprise when my teenage daughter, who avows that she'd rather be out and about shopping for Prada any day than in the garden and wouldn't be seen dead in a vegetable patch, will proudly dig up and

OPPOSITE: Garlic drying, before being ready to be strung for storage.

show off vegetables that 'we've' grown when her friends are around, and even though she has a bird phobia, she will happily take her sleepover friends off for an egg hunt at breakfast time.

Joining the garden farming fraternity

Because the knowledge of previous generations about how to keep a garden farm has disappeared, it's quite common to find that your parents don't know anything about gardening, so you may need to gain experience and knowledge from your local community. You'll discover a great deal of camaraderie when keeping a garden farm. Experienced gardeners will be more than happy to share their experiences and advice with you. I have met some fascinating and extraordinary people through growing vegetables and keeping animals; people who've freely given their time, knowledge and even some of their prize vegetables or eggs just for the joy of sharing. What I've learned is that there is always something more to learn. Even gardeners who have grown produce or kept animals all their lives are still keen to hear of your experiences that, in turn, may help them, no matter how trivial or small.

In my neighbourhood, we frequently swap our produce – a glut of courgettes, potatoes or beetroot is often exchanged for jars of honey, jam or chutney, or eggs, and if you have to go away or need a holiday, the contacts you make will be invaluable when you need someone to look after your animals or water the garden.

It's always good to make contact with your local gardening or poultry club or beekeeping society; some of the latter will even match you up with a 'buddy' for a couple of years to help you start your bee colony. You will gain a great sense of community, and may even go on to enter some of your produce or show some of your livestock and win prizes at a local show.

Gaining inspiration and restoration

Your garden farm will be a place where you'll feel calm, and recharge and restore your sanity from the pressures of 21st-century living. Some of your efforts will be hit and miss, and there'll be some mistakes, but you'll soon discover that, with a little help from the elements, your seeds and young plants will flourish along with your enthusiasm and confidence, and you'll be set up with a way of life that there's no going back on.

From being out in the fresh air, you will increase your sense of awareness of nature and the seasons. Recently, when I was with my family looking for blackberries, we came across a whole abundance of wildlife we weren't expecting that day: a bird's nest full of little fledglings hidden in a hedgerow, a greengage bush laden with ripe fruits, a squirrel foraging for nuts and a deer family bounding through the woods, barely making a sound as they swept through the trees. These are pleasures we would never have experienced if we'd decided to stay in.

OPPOSITE: When planning the space between your vegetable beds, ensure there is enough room for a wheelbarrow.

CHAPTER ONE

Starting Off

When you've made the decision to be a garden farmer, knowing just how to begin can be daunting, as there's so much choice on offer in garden centres and seed catalogues. The secret is in the planning: go to the shop or browse the catalogue with a list. Think about what types of produce you want to grow – what vegetables you eat, the space you have available and the time you can commit are all factors in narrowing down the choice. When starting out there'll be a lot of trial and error involved.

Don't let the fear of not having the right equipment put you off. It's surprising what you'll uncover in your own garden shed. There are many tools available, including a variety of fancy gadgets, but all you need to begin with are the basics – a garden fork, a trowel and a watering can.

Cost doesn't have to be an issue. A packet of seeds is surprisingly cheap. You'll need a few bags of compost to start off your seed trays, and for the first year, until you've created your garden compost, it's useful to buy in some well-rotted manure to enrich your soil. Alternatively, you may have a local farmer or neighbour who keeps animals who'll be able to provide some for free in exchange for some of your garden produce.

Vegetables are very willing companions. The seeds will want to germinate and the plants will be more than enthusiastic to grow. Don't be put off by pests and diseases either; they're often less troublesome than you think. Yes, you may lose a few plants along the way, but with experience you'll find the best methods and controls. Starting off with a vegetable garden is one of the most enjoyable things in life, and with a little thought and planning, you'll be set up for the foreseeable future.

PLANNING YOUR KITCHEN GARDEN
Food for thought

When spring comes, it's easy to get overexcited by the array of seed packets on the shelves of your local garden centre or in mail order catalogues. Vegetables are anything but ugly, and a well-planted vegetable garden is a beautiful sight. The different sizes, shapes, colours and textures of the leaves and crop give your garden a rich, abundant and welcoming atmosphere.

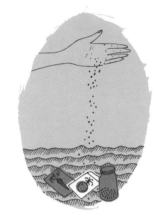

What to plant

The joy of simply growing vegetables can result in vegetable beds full of plants that you and your family don't eat. Prepare a list of vegetables you want to grow and arrange the crops in the garden according to the amounts you wish to grow, dates to be planted and the available space. Plant tall crops on the north side of the garden so that they don't shade low-growing crops. Careful planning will ensure that you have a continuous crop of vegetables all year round. Keep a record in either a garden notebook or on your computer of what varieties and how many you have planted, how well they have grown and when and what you've harvested. This will come in very useful when planning next season's planting.

Talk to local farmers or gardening societies about what crops they grow and when they plant and harvest them. Ask about your local first and last frost dates, and schedule your sowing and planting accordingly.

Plot position

Vegetable beds are best sited on level ground and I've always tried to position them as near as possible to the house. Beds that are out of sight are often more neglected, and if visible from indoors, it's much easier to spot when an escaped chicken

is raiding your lovingly grown, tender spinach. I once had a vegetable bed around the corner and out of eyeshot of the house. On my usual rounds during the evening I found a whole row of young leaves pecked to the ground by a fat chicken escapee who'd been happily nibbling out of sight all day.

Space

Plant according to your space, as well as soil type and local climate. Some vegetables such as artichokes and cabbages require a lot of space and are slow growing, which means they'll take up valuable room all season. If you have a small area or a patio, make use of planting in pots and containers (see pages 51–52), grow plenty of the vegetables you know you'll eat and avoid tying up valuable space by growing just one plant that will take months to grow and that you may not eat.

When a space appears in your vegetable plot, be ready to fill it with another crop. Choose high-yielding varieties and fast-growing crops; salad leaves, for example, are perfect for filling in gaps. If you sow replacement crops in small pots, they will be ready to transplant into the vegetable patch as soon as the space becomes available.

Use trellises, stakes or cages made from wood or garden twine to support vining crops such as tomato, squash, cucumber and pole beans that use up a great deal of space when allowed to grow along the ground, thus minimizing the use of ground space and increasing garden productivity.

Early-maturing, quick-growing crops such as beans, radishes, onions, spinach, rocket or salad leaves can be planted between the rows of late-maturing crops like tomatoes, peppers, cabbage or sweetcorn to increase production in a small area, the former being harvested before the others become large and block out the sun.

Water

In the summer months when watering is a daily ritual, having access to an outside tap or hosepipe will save a lot of heaving of watering cans to and from the house. Make sure that you have a hosepipe long enough to reach your beds and greenhouse or cold frame. Plan your vegetable

BELOW: Planting salad leaves makes good use of space between rows of other vegetables.

garden away from waterlogged areas and aim for a position where the soil is well drained.

If possible, make a separate area for your beds away from tree roots and shady shrubs that will compete with the vegetables for the moisture available in the soil.

Weather

Avoid windy spots. Wind will slow down growth and can damage some of the taller, more fragile plants such as broad beans and sweetcorn. If unavoidable, consider planting small hedges or fences around your vegetable area, but they must be far enough away and low enough not to create too much shade. Your crops will grow best in as much sun as possible, although some plants will prefer a little shade in the hotter months. Vegetables need at least six hours of sunlight each day for optimum growth. Bear in mind that the angle of the sun is lower in the spring and autumn, and may affect how the garden is shaded by nearby trees.

Gluts

Thinking carefully about which vegetables you will eat in the largest quantities and planting accordingly will avoid gluts and wasted effort in growing produce that ends up overripe and thrown onto the compost. If you find yourself with more of one type of vegetable than you or your family can eat, think about getting together with neighbours or friends and do a vegetable share. In my neighbourhood, we'll often be seen wandering around each other's gardens at dinner time, wielding a knife, scissors or secateurs, collecting different vegetables from each one. Some of us prefer planting ornamental cabbages, while others grow more salad leaves or different varieties of carrot. We're all very keen to share our gluts rather than bin them and it makes for a wonderful community spirit and friendly competitiveness over whose are the best plants.

Wildlife

Most wildlife is an asset to the kitchen gardener: hedgehogs eat a range of garden pests, foxes take mice and frogs will consume slugs. Having said that, some birds, particularly pigeons, can be a nuisance and will devour leafy seedlings, while mice can be troublesome if they get to your fresh, ripe strawberries before you do.

Crop rotation

A particular crop of vegetables should not be grown in the same spot each year, so it's essential to rotate your crops on a three- or four-year cycle. Rotating your vegetables will avoid pests and diseases and prevent the soil nutrients becoming unbalanced.

Rotating takes a little planning as well as a basic knowledge of the vegetable families. Vegetables are categorized into basic family groups (see panel below), and these groups of vegetables should be rotated together, as they use soil in similar ways and share similar pests. Most vegetables are hardy or semi-hardy annuals and should be planted every year on a four-year rotation so that the same vegetable family isn't planted in the same location within four years.

Vegetable families

Roots Potatoes, carrots, beetroot, radishes, parsnips

Brassicas Cabbage, broccoli, Brussels sprouts, cauliflower, kale

Legumes Peas, beans

Onions Garlic, leeks, onions, shallots

Cucurbits Squashes, pumpkins, courgettes, marrows, melons, cucumbers

Stem and perennial veg Celery, celeriac, fennel, artichokes, asparagus, rhubarb

Fruiting veg Tomatoes, peppers, chillies, sweetcorn

Leaves and salads Lettuce, mustard cress, radicchio, chicory, endive, rocket, spinach, chard

ABOVE: *An example of crop rotation. Clockwise from top left: root veg, brassicas, legumes, onions – rotate the beds annually.*

Companion planting

The concept of companion planting is that if you plant certain plants around or close to others, they can offer them the benefit of providing pest control without the need to use chemicals. Some combinations work because of the scents the plants use to repel insects, others by attracting beneficial pests or acting as a decoy for harmful ones. Through combining plants carefully, you can create plant communities that also help each other by providing nutrients in the soil or offering protection from wind or sun. Companion planting isn't a new idea – gardeners have used it for a long time – but debate continues as to whether or not it works. Whatever your view, it's worth trying this method if you're having particular problems growing one type of vegetable or if you've been unsuccessful in getting rid of pests using organic methods. Use this chart as a guide to planting companion plants that will either attract pollinators or pest predators to help your plants thrive.

Plant	Companions	Function
Apple	Nasturtium, chives	Nasturtium climbs tree and repels codling moth. Chives grown beneath apple trees will help to prevent apple scab.
Asparagus	Parsley	Helps improve flavour.
Avocados	Comfrey	Great natural compost and nutrient provider.
Bean	Rosemary, sweetcorn	Rosemary deters bean beetles. Sweetcorn acts as a trellis for beans and beans attract predators of corn pests.
Beetroot	Onion, lettuce, cabbage, garlic	Adds minerals to the soil if leaves are left to compost in the ground.
Brassicas (cabbage, cauliflower, broccoli)	Aromatic plants, sage, dill, chamomile, beetroot, peppermint, rosemary, bean, onion, potato, garlic, mint	Dill attracts parasitic wasps to control cabbage butterfly. Rosemary, mint and garlic deter cabbage butterfly. Chamomile deters flies and mosquitoes and gives strength to plants growing nearby.
Carrot	Lettuce, pea, leek, chives, onion, cucumber, bean, tomato, sage, rosemary	Tomatoes grow well with carrots, but can reduce the carrots' growth. Beans provide nitrogen that carrots need more than some other vegetables. Aromatic companion plants tend to repel carrot fly, as does leek.

Plant	Companions	Function
Celery	Leek	Improves growth.
Courgette, cucumber	French marigold, bean, sweetcorn, pea, radish	Marigolds are a particularly good companion for most plants. They produce a strong pesticidal chemical from their roots. Radish deters cucumber beetles and rust flies.
Fruit trees	Tansy, comfrey	Tansy is a good general insect repellent, as well as of ants and mice, and is a useful addition to the compost pile, as it's high in potassium. Warning: don't plant it near livestock, as it's toxic to many animals.
Lettuce	Tall flowers, carrots, radish, onion family	Flowers offer light shade for lettuce. Onion helps improve flavour.
Onion	Leek, chamomile	Leek improves growth. Chamomile deters flies and mosquitoes and gives strength to plants growing nearby.
Potato	Beans, cabbage, marigold, horseradish, sweetcorn	Horseradish, planted at the corners of the potato patch, provides general protection. Don't plant tomatoes and potatoes together, as they can both get early and late blight and can contaminate each other.
Pumpkin	Sweetcorn, squash, marigold, nasturtium, oregano	Marigold deters beetles. Nasturtium deters bugs and beetles. Oregano provides general pest protection.
Raspberries	Garlic	Helps keep aphids away from raspberries.
Spinach	Radish	Radish attracts leaf miner away from spinach.
Squash	Borage	Improves growth and flavour.
Strawberry	Onion, garlic, borage	All help to improve flavour. Onions help the berries fight disease. Borage increases the yield.

Plant	Companions	Function
Tomato	French marigold, borage, onion, garlic, parsley, asparagus, chives, broccoli, sweet basil, marigold, carrots	Marigolds repel whitefly when planted with tomatoes. Borage deters tomato worm and improves growth and flavour. Onion, garlic and parsley help to improve flavour. Planting basil in the greenhouse with tomatoes helps repel flies and aphids. Mint deters ants and fleas (especially spearmint) and will deter clothes moths.
Most plants	Marigold	Repels carrot flies and is a general insect repellent.
Most plants, particularly radishes, brassicas, cucurbits, fruit trees	Nasturtium	Secretes a mustard oil, which many insects find attractive, particularly the cabbage white moth. The flowers repel aphids and the cucumber beetle. The climbing variety grown up apple trees will repel codling moth.
Most plants	Nettle	Beneficial anywhere; increases aroma and pungency of herbs
Most plants	Fennel	Repels flies, fleas and ants.
Most plants	Peas	Peas fix nitrogen in the soil. Plant with sweetcorn, bean, carrot, cucumber, parsley, early potato, radish, spinach, strawberry, pepper. Do not plant peas with onions.
Most plants	Sunflower	Plant sunflowers around the garden to deter aphids. Ants will drive aphids onto sunflowers. The aphids will cause little damage to the sunflowers.
Most plants	Thyme	Protects brassicas, improves growth and flavour of vegetables; general insect repellent.
Most plants	Catnip	Repels fleas, ants and rodents.

SOIL
Ground rules

Soil is the most important resource in your kitchen garden. The type and condition of the soil that you have influences the crops that you grow. If you look after your soil well, feed it and nurture it, it will look after your vegetables, which in turn will look after you.

Composition

Soil is made up of organic matter: bacteria, fungi and tiny creatures that recycle the organic matter and use the air, moisture and the minerals to make essential plant food. Well-balanced soil contains equal amounts of three types of particle: sand, silt and clay. Clay has the smallest soil particles, silt has medium-sized particles and sand has the coarsest particles. The amounts of clay, silt and sand in a soil determine its texture. Loam, the ideal garden soil, is a mixture of 20 per cent clay, 40 per cent silt and 40 per cent sand.

Soil varies greatly from area to area and sometimes one type of particle is dominant (see chart below). If this is the case with your soil, it will benefit from some help from you to get the best out of your vegetable plants. Soils that have been uncultivated for years are often deficient in one or other of the elements necessary for healthy plants. A medium soil, well supplied with organic material, is ideal for most vegetables. It is open, easily worked, warms up quickly and retains moisture in summer.

What's your soil type?

Sandy	Dry and gritty; runs easily through your fingers. It drains easily in winter and warms up well in the spring. It doesn't hold many nutrients and can dry out quickly in summer.
Clay	Sticky; when squeezed into a ball it keeps its shape and can be moulded into other shapes. It will cake as it dries, making it unsuitable for young plants. Rich in nutrients, drains badly in winter, but will usually stay moist in summer.
Silty	Silky in feel; neither squeezes into a ball nor falls readily through the fingers. Easily damaged during the winter. It's a fertile soil and is relatively unlikely to be found in gardens.
Loamy	Crumbly; in between clay and sand. This is the best soil to have in the garden.
Chalky	Alkaline and fast draining, requiring extra watering and nutrients.
Peaty	Dark, spongy and organically rich – wonderfully fertile, but usually acidic.

Soil pH

Soil is either acid, neutral or alkaline, depending on the amount of calcium in the soil, which is measured using the pH scale. This ranges from 1.0 to 14.0; a pH of 7.0 is neutral, 1.0–7.0 is acidic and 7.0–14.0 is alkaline. As a general guide, vegetables will grow best in a slightly acid soil with a pH of 6.5. Some vegetables have more specific needs; for example, the cabbage family favours a pH of 7–7.5, which helps reduce club root disease, potatoes like acid soil, whereas brassicas prefer alkaline soil.

An acidic soil contains too little calcium, an alkaline soil too much. With too little calcium, nutrients wash out of the soil; with too much, nutrients are trapped in the soil and can't be absorbed by the plants.

It's useful to measure the pH of your soil and you can buy home soil test kits from good gardening stores to give you a quick indication of the level of its acidity or alkalinity so that you can make the necessary adjustments (see below). The solution in the kit will usually turn orangey yellow in the case of an acid soil and dark green with an alkaline soil.

If your soil is acid, you can spread garden lime on top and then mix it into the soil enough to raise the pH level.

Testing the pH levels of your soil

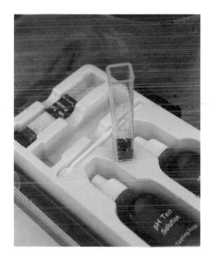

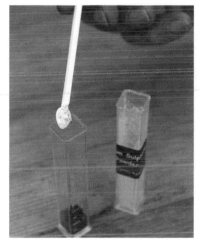

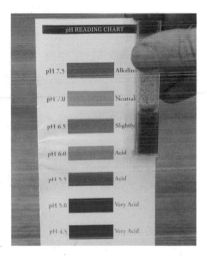

1 Remove the top 5 cm (2 in) of soil and remove it to one side. Break up the soil underneath and dig to approximately 12 cm (5 in). Place some of the lower-level soil in a pot, remove all twigs, stones and any bugs, and leave to dry naturally.

2 Put some of the dry soil into the tube of your testing kit up to the 1 ml mark. Add one scoop of the barium sulphate. Fill the tube to the 2.5 ml mark with the pH test solution.

3 Replace the cap and shake the tube. Leave the contents to settle for around 10 minutes. Hold the tube up against the colour chart to determine the pH level of your soil.

Improving your soil

Soil is alive and needs to be treated as a living substance. Putting some extra effort into preparing your soil before planting will save you a lot of time and effort in the future.

Dig your vegetable bed to break up compacted soil (this will help with drainage) and remove rocks, weeds and stones. Try to pull out as much of the weed roots as possible or they will keep returning. Don't tread on soil if it's too wet, as this will compact it and damage the soil's structure.

Compost and other supplements can be added to any type of soil to improve its structure and this will enhance the size, flavour and yield of your vegetables. The long-term objective of soil improvement is to build up humus, which is the organic matter that remains after the decomposition of plant and animal residues.

As a guide, add one bucketful of well-rotted organic matter – see opposite for the different types you can use – to every square metre (yard). If you have thin or poor soil, double this amount. Spread the organic matter on top of the soil and then mix it into the top 15–30 cm (6–12 in), digging it in with a spade. This can be very hard labour, so plan to work on small areas at a time and possibly over a few days. Don't worry if your bed is a few centimetres (inches) higher when you've finished – the level will settle over the course of the season. Add more organic matter twice yearly.

Drainage can also be improved by loosening the soil through cultivation. There are several common misconceptions about improving clay soil, for instance that adding sand will loosen it up and improve it, but in reality this will probably make the soil harder and cement-like.

LEFT: As well as benefiting the soil, digging the garden is great exercise, but remember to take frequent breaks.

Which organic matter?

Compost Collecting your garden and kitchen waste and making your own compost is by far the cheapest and best option (see pages 24–27).

Manure Well-rotted horse manure is excellent, as is chicken manure from your own garden. If you don't keep hens and you collect hen waste from a local battery or broiler hen farm, ensure that this is well rotted down before using it, as it will contain all the chemicals that are given to the battery hens. According to some researchers, when they applied 10 tonnes (tons) per 0.4 hectare (1 acre) of chicken broiler litter and 1 tonne (ton) per 0.4 hectare (1 acre) of lime in the autumn, they found that they achieved 20 per cent higher yields in the next summer's tomato crop as well as larger and earlier-maturing fruit.

Manure should always be composted until it turns dark and crumbly. Fresh manure contains ammonia that can burn your plants.

BELOW: Raised beds are an excellent way of managing your vegetable and herb beds.

Grass clippings or shredded leaves Work into the soil so that it decomposes slowly.

Green manures Also known as a 'cover crop', these are grown to improve the soil. If green manures are grown in the autumn or winter, they will stop the nutrients from being washed away from the soil and suppress weeds. The roots will also keep the structure loose. Legumes (peas and beans) are good plants for green manures, as they decay quickly because their residues are high in nitrogen. Grass crops, such as rye, will also have a beneficial effect on soil organic matter because they have a high carbon to nitrogen ratio and decay more slowly. If allowed to flower, some green manures will attract pollinating insects. Other green manure crops include mustard, fenugreek, lupin, alfalfa and buckwheat.

Green manure seeds are sown directly into the soil. The plants are then dug in when they are lush and leafy, but before flowering. Allow at least two weeks after digging the manures into the soil before planting or sowing.

COMPOSTING
Putting something back

There is a very good reason for composting. Every household produces waste that can be turned into a completely free and renewable source of nutrients to improve your soil and provide your plants with an excellent boost. It's an energy-efficient method of using up your vegetable matter and an excellent way to recycle.

How it works

Composting is the end product of the decomposition of organic matter. To make compost, you simply combine a mixture of kitchen scraps such as peelings and raw vegetable matter, garden waste, manure, leaves, grass clippings, cardboard and straw. This will all naturally decompose and, if properly managed, will provide a rich organic matter that will be perfect for your garden. In a healthy compost pile you'll find fine moulds, bacteria, fungi, earthworms, mites and beetles. These are not garden pests and won't overrun your garden.

To make compost, simply create a pile in the corner of your garden, or contain the ingredients within a wooden container (see pages 26–27) or a bought plastic bin. Compost bins are easy and cheap to buy, often subsidized by your local authority in a bid to encourage all households to compost and reduce landfill sites.

Composting needs alternate layers of wet and dry material. Wet material is high in nitrogen and low in carbon, and helps to break down dry material, which is low in nitrogen and high in carbon.

RIGHT: When made from recycled railway sleepers or wood, compost bins look attractive and hold the compost in well.

Creating your own compost

Find an area in your garden that is flat and put your compost bin directly onto the soil so that any liquid waste can simply drain away. It's also essential that worms can get up into the compost through the soil underneath.

Grass clippings are a common compost ingredient, so depending how large your lawn is, it's sometimes useful to make a separate section for the clippings to keep them in one place ready to add to the compost in layers.

recipe for success

Think of making compost like a recipe and the secret of success is to create the right mixture. To achieve this, first divide your ingredients, or composting material, into two categories:

GREENS Quick to rot, these release moisture and nitrogen. They include fruit waste, tea bags, uncooked vegetable scraps, plant prunings, nettles and grass cuttings.

BROWNS Slower to rot and also allow air pockets to form in the mixture. They include cardboard, fallen leaves, egg boxes, eggshells and scrunched-up paper.

KEEP OUT Some items should never be put on the compost including meat, dairy products, cooked vegetables, diseased plants, pet faeces or baby's nappies. These can attract unwanted pests such as rats and also create a nasty smell.

There are also some weeds that you don't want to add, such as thistles, dandelions or anything with seed heads.

Don't add plastic bottles, metal, cans or glass – these should all be put in their respective recycling facilities.

The greens and the browns should be perfectly balanced in layers. If the compost is looking wet, you need to add some more browns; if the compost looks too dry, you need to add more greens. It's a good idea to keep a check on the moisture level and water the compost with a watering can if it gets too dry.

Aerating and maturing

The compost also needs to have lots of air in it in order to feed the bacteria. Try adding scrunched-up cardboard, or aerate the compost with a fork or special aerator tool to create deep air pockets. But the best results are produced by turning the compost. If it's contained in open wooden boxes (see opposite), turn it by forking the compost from one bin to the other. If using a plastic bin, simply lift it off the compost and fork the compost back into the bin, repeating three or four times within a six-month period. It's best to use two bins at a time so that you can leave one to mature while still adding to the other.

When the compost container is full, cover it with an old thick blanket, mats, carpet or a rainproof lid. In six to nine months your compost will be ready for the garden.

Accessing and applying

When you are ready to use the compost, use the matter from the bottom and remove any decomposing matter that may still be left into the second bin. The mature compost can then be sprinkled over or dug into your vegetable beds. You'll be amazed at how much your plants will thrive and highly satisfied to know that you've created this rich plant food with your everyday domestic waste.

ABOVE: Treat compost as you would a r[...] and add several layers of ingredients.

BELOW: If you have the space, build sev[...] compost bins to make raking over and [...] turning the compost easier.

making a reclaimed compost bin

Wooden pallets are frequently discarded and left to fill up landfill sites, but they are perfect for making compost bins. They are often free and all you'll need to turn them into an ideal compost bin are a few basic DIY materials and tools.

1 Use wood screws or baling wire to join three upright wooden pallets together to form three sides of a square.

2 Attach sliding bolts to the front edge of the bin and the last pallet to make a removable door at the front, or attach turn buttons to the front edge of the bin.

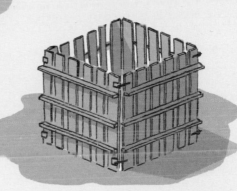

3 If you have enough space, it's best to make a three-bin system by joining on two additional sets of pallets in a row, with a door for each – you will need 10 pallets in total. Start off your compost in one bin and then gradually turn the compost into the next bin every few weeks.

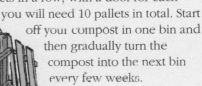

WORMERIES
Another way with waste

A wormery is simply a box containing composting worms that you supply with ordinary kitchen waste, which the worms then eat and turn into a rich and valuable liquid feed that can be mixed into the soil as compost or mulch. It will usually have a tap to drain off the liquid or layers that you can remove and use as compost. Wormeries are available to buy, but you can also easily build your own (see opposite).

Composting worms

This particular type of worm lives and feeds near the surface, unlike garden earthworms that burrow deeper into the soil. Composting worms should be fed on kitchen scraps and will eat both cooked and uncooked waste – they eat almost anything that will decompose and can consume half or all their own weight in waste each day. Prolific breeders, they self-regulate their population to the available space and the amount of food, providing a continuous, plentiful supply for your wormery. Brandling or tiger composting worms can be obtained from a mature compost heap or they can be purchased.

Wormery dos and don'ts

DO
- ✔ Feed vegetables, vegetable peelings, onions (restricted amounts), citrus fruits (restricted amounts), fruit and fruit peel, coffee grains and tea bags/leaves, cereals, bread, rice, pasta, crushed eggshells, flowers, cakes, biscuits, sugar, cheese (restricted amounts), meat and fish (restricted amounts), cardboard, paper, pet or human hair, vacuum cleaner contents, pet faeces (vegetarian animals only), leaves.

- ✔ Try to vary the diet of your worms; they prefer a mixture of kitchen scraps.

- ✔ Place the wormery somewhere sheltered; it may be best inside a shed in the winter for protection, or insulate it by wrapping carpet or bubblewrap around the outside. Keep out of direct sunlight in the summer and away from strong winds.

DON'T
- ✘ Feed garlic, spicy foods, dairy products, salt, oil, grass cuttings, bones, eggs, weeds, insecticides or pesticides, paint, non-biodegradable material, solvents, soaps, cosmetics or detergents, chicken manure, poisonous plants, diseased plant material.

- ✘ Give them excess amounts of meat or fish, otherwise it could attract rats and make the wormery smell bad.

- ✘ Overfeed your worms or they may die, so don't add more waste until the previous waste has been composted.

- ✘ Allow your worms to get too hot or cold, or they may die; worm activity will cease below 10°C (50°F).

building your own wormery

1 Drill several drainage holes on the outside of a plastic dustbin about 5 cm (2 in) up from the base and 25 cm (10 in) apart. Drill a circle of air holes 5 cm (2 in) from the top of the bin.

2 Fill the bin with an 8–10-cm (3–4-in) layer of coarse sand or gravel. Add a round of wood or polythene with holes drilled for drainage.

3 Add a 7–8-cm (2¾–3-in) layer of moistened bedding material; well-rotted compost or manure works well. Place at least 100 composting worms in the bedding.

4 Add 1 litre (1¾ pints) of chopped-up kitchen waste on one side of the bin. Cover with well-soaked newspaper.

5 Replace the lid and leave the worms undisturbed for at least two to three weeks to settle into their new home. Add more kitchen waste when the previous addition has been composted.

6 Keep the bin covered with a lid to avoid fruit flies. It will take two to three months for the worms to process the food and turn it into liquid that you'll be able to drain off.

Wormery troubleshooting

If the compost is looking soggy and wet, this may indicate that you're overfeeding the worms. Stir up any uneaten food, as this will provide some oxygen, and try adding some brown material (cardboard or dry paper).

If the compost is looking too dry, add some water and stir in some green material.

If in the first few days of starting your wormery the worms attempt to escape, this is because they're not yet used to their new environment. Try adding some garden soil, which is full of tiny creatures and organisms and will help acclimatize your worms. When they are used to their new home, they will stay where the food is.

GROWING IN RAISED BEDS
Well contained and maintained

By far the best option of managing your kitchen garden is to use raised beds for growing your vegetables. These are specially constructed, contained areas – basically a box without a base to hold in the soil – where the soil surface is higher than the ground, making for easy access, maintenance and organization.

Design considerations

The sides of the bed can be made of wood, stone or brick, depending on your preferred style. They can be built at a low level or higher to make gardening easier, but higher beds will need more soil. They should be no wider than 1.2 m (4 ft) so that you can reach the centre of the bed from both sides. The optimum length is 3 m (10 ft).

ABOVE: Plant your herbs near the house and when you brush past you'll enjoy the delicious scent.

When planning a raised bed, make sure that you make the pathways wide enough to accommodate a wheelbarrow and that there is adequate draining so that the paths don't get waterlogged in the winter.

The pros and cons of raised beds

PROS

✔ Crops are all concentrated in one area and are easier to weed

✔ Easy access from paths in between each bed

✔ Easier to manage crop rotation (see page 16)

✔ The soil warms up quickly and drains well

✔ Easy to manage the soil in a concentrated area

✔ The beds can be filled with the appropriate type of soil for your crops

✔ Vegetables are grown in short rows, thus making gluts less likely

✔ Cloches, fleeces, netting and supports are easier to manage

✔ Reclaimed materials can be used to create the sides

✔ The beds can accommodate large or small areas

✔ Their compact size means that you don't have to tread or compact the soil

✔ They look great!

CONS

✘ The initial potential expense of setting up and constructing the beds

✘ The soil dries out more quickly

✘ The structures are permanent

making a wooden raised bed

1 Mark out the area where you plan to have your raised beds and cut your timber planks to size. It's a good idea to measure the areas out using canes or sprinkled flour in order to check that it fits in with your plan and adjust as necessary. Clear the soil where you have planned your beds and get rid of any weeds or existing plants.

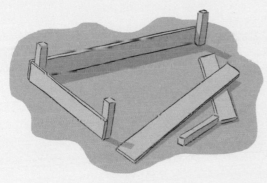

2 You will need four 10 x 10-cm (4 x 4-in) thick posts, one for each corner of the bed, cut to length according to the depth of your bed sides plus 15 cm (6 in) for sinking into the ground.

3 Attach the wooden planking to the posts using galvanized screws.

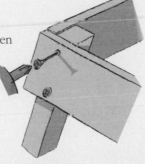

4 Hammer the corner posts into the ground. Turn over the soil in the ground of the bed area before filling it by at least one-third with well-rotted compost. Top up with soil taken from other parts of the garden.

> **Tip:** Choose untreated wood to avoid any chemicals leaking into the soil and damaging your crops.

EQUIPMENT
Kitting up for action

I'm sure that cultivating tools were the first things that man ever owned. Tools will be your constant companions around the garden farm, so get to know and love them. Also vital in even the smallest garden is a shed to keep your tools and hen- and beekeeping equipment safe and dry.

Sheds

If you are well and truly dedicated to your garden farm, your shed will need to be bigger than most garden sheds and divided into sections. Storage of any animal feed should, if possible, be kept in galvanized steel bins to keep out rats and other pests. You may want more than one shed; one for gardening and one for your animal-keeping equipment.

The shed should be waterproof and secure, and large enough for your needs. Use the space wisely. For example, hooks for hanging up gardening tools and organized shelving will save you valuable time in the cold of winter when the last thing you want to do is spend half an hour looking for your garden fork. Ensure that the shed has electricity and is easily accessible.

Sheds are a gardener's retreat, so keep it comfortably tidy and make space for a seat – you'll need a well-earned rest.

OPPOSITE: You don't need to spend a fortune on pristine new tools – well-kept, second-hand tools will do a great job.

Tools

There are only a few essential tools that you'll need to help you succeed in making and maintaining your kitchen garden, but whichever you decide to buy, make sure that they are the best quality you can afford. Some good-quality tools come with interchangeable handles and heads, which will save on costs. Purchase from a company that guarantees against problems or defects and has a satisfaction guarantee. If you're buying on the internet, this is particularly important, as you won't be able to pick up the items and assess their weight or balance before making a choice.

You can also buy good-quality second-hand tools at markets. Gardeners are usually very conscientious about their tools and will keep them in good condition, so it's worth searching around for a good find.

Start with the basics and then build up your collection over time. It's better to start off with a few basic, quality tools than lots of cheap tools that won't do the job or will make the work more difficult for you.

Essential tool kit

Spade Used for digging and turning over soil and dividing. Regularly clean and sharpen your spade and it will last you a lifetime.

Fork For loosening up soil and incorporating compost or manure. Vital for digging up potatoes, a potato fork is purpose-designed with flatter prongs so that you're less likely to spike one of your precious potatoes.

Trowel Most vegetable gardening seems to take place on your knees with a trowel in hand. Narrow blades are good for digging deeper holes when planting out and wider blades are best for moving soil around. Steel blades will last longer and are well worth the investment.

Hoe Used for weeding and keeping the soil loose. A Dutch hoe is used with a pushing motion with the blade just below the soil surface, and is good for dragging backwards, leaving the soil free from footprints. A draw hoe is a fast way of clearing weeds, penetrating deeper into the soil to remove tougher weeds.

Watering can Choose one as big as possible, but not so big that you can't carry it. The galvanized ones will last longer, but they're heavier to carry. I keep my seedlings on quite high ledges and therefore have to lift my watering can to reach them, making a lighter plastic one the right choice, so select what's appropriate for your needs. One that comes with different grades of rose is advisable.

Secateurs A good, sharp pair of secateurs should go with you everywhere in the garden, used for

LEFT: Look out for vintage tools; if well kept, they will work just as well as sparkling new ones for you.

trimming down plants, deadheading and harvesting herbs and vegetables. They are quicker to use than a knife.

Pruning knife Excellent for a variety of jobs around the garden farm, from opening sacks of chicken feed to harvesting crops. A 'must-have' in the pocket of every garden farmer, no matter how large or small your garden.

Dibber Purpose designed ones can be bought, but equally they can be made from old wooden handles. The smaller ones are particularly useful when sowing seeds and transplanting them.

> **Tip:** I use the broken end of an old knitting needle as a dibber when planting out my seedlings. Knitting needles or crochet hooks are great for this purpose because they come in all different thicknesses.

Rake A large steel rake is ideal for using on seedbeds and covering seeds.

Garden line Used in vegetable beds for measuring out straight lines. Custom-made lines are perfect because they swivel on the reel and are easy to use. Alternatively, use some string attached to a piece of cane.

Buckets and baskets Large plastic gardener's buckets in a multitude of colours are great to have around the garden for collecting weeds and moving soil and plants around, and are generally useful containers. Use baskets for collecting harvested crops to bring back to the kitchen – they will make you especially proud of your beautiful-looking produce.

Wheelbarrow Your wheelbarrow needs to be strong enough to carry soil, compost, manure and chicken waste. There are now strong yet lightweight plastic or steel wheelbarrows available. The tyre needs to be strong, the more expensive the wheelbarrow, the less likely you are to have a tyre puncture.

Gardening gloves Lots of gardening will give you sore hands if you don't look after them. Gloves are necessary to protect your hands from sharp branches and stinging weeds. Also wear gloves when doing heavy work and particularly during the cold weather. There are plenty of varieties available – buy those that suit you and your budget best.

Kneeler Most of your time in the garden will be spent kneeling and you can get sore or damp knees. Buy a kneeler that is waterproof and sturdy enough not to rip easily. Kneelers vary hugely from simple pads to benches that aid getting up and down.

Tool TLC

If you take care of your tools, they'll take care of you.

Clean your tools regularly. Remove any soil that's been left on the ends of blades and handles, which can harden if left over time.

Remove any rust on blades as soon as it appears.

Rub down wooden handles with fine-grade sandpaper and then rub in linseed oil.

Gather up all tools and equipment at the end of each day and store somewhere safe and dry.

Lock tools in a shed; they are valuable equipment and are prone to theft.

At the end of the season, give your tools a service by cleaning and sharpening them.

CHAPTER TWO

Sowing and Growing

Once you've made your plan, it's now time to jump in and begin. When I first started out I frequently went to my local garden centre to buy seeds, only to walk out with nothing at all because I was overwhelmed by the amount of varieties of each plant. Enjoy searching for seeds or small plants in the catalogues and garden shops and don't be put off by the abundant varieties available; just choose one you like and take the plunge.

Planting seeds and looking after seedlings is a truly satisfying experience. It will certainly bring out your nurturing instincts – you'll constantly be checking to see if they've germinated and you won't be able to contain your excitement when you see them all bursting through the soil.

In this chapter there are tips on how to sow seeds, look after your young seedlings, when and how to water to get the best results and even how to make your own natural fertilizer from your own garden using nettles.

Don't let the pests and diseases get you down – they really aren't all that bad. Once you begin to recognize them, you'll be able to act accordingly, and if you've treated your plants well and they are happy and healthy, they'll have their own defences to fight them off.

You will be entering into a partnership with your plants – they will want to thrive for you and in the following pages you'll find out how you can best help nature on its way.

GROWING UNDER COVER
A nurturing environment

This doesn't mean you have to wear a dark suit, dress in disguise or only go into the garden during the night! Growing under cover means you can garden whatever the weather outside, either on your kitchen windowsill, in a greenhouse, polytunnel or cold frame or under a cloche, enabling you to sow crops early or grow unusual crops that you wouldn't be able to do in your own local climate.

Kitchen windowsills

These are a great advantage when starting off seedlings, allowing you to watch them emerge and grow until they're big enough, when you can transfer them into a greenhouse or cold frame before planting outside.

ABOVE: *A windowsill is the perfect environment for young seedlings and for enjoying the scent of fresh basil.*

Greenhouse guidelines

Size Assess the greenhouse size in relation to your growing requirements and the available space in your garden, bearing in mind that it will need a sunny, flat site.

Even the smallest greenhouse can be an asset to your garden, but a useful size is 2.4 m (8 ft) long by 1.8 m (6 ft) wide. Ensure that the door is tightly fitting; sliding doors make it easier to adjust the ventilation and take up less space. Check that the height is going to give you adequate headroom – greenhouses generally have sloping sides, so are higher in the middle.

Position The greenhouse should receive the maximum amount of winter sunlight available. If setting it up in the winter when trees and shrubs are bare, take into account how much leafier and shadier they will be in the summer.

If possible, set up your greenhouse with the long side facing south, as the angle of the roof is designed to catch the maximum amount of the sun's rays in the winter with the least amount of loss by reflection, and if your greenhouse requires some shading over the summer, you will only need to shade one side.

Space Plan the greenhouse well, making sure that there is adequate space on the floor for a pathway and enough space to place grow bags and shelves.

You'll need enough space to be able to move around comfortably and for potting plants. Potting benches can be bought that fold down when not in use, which are usually slotted so that spilled soil can fall into a collection bin below.

Brackets and hooks are useful either for supporting hanging baskets or hanging tools and equipment, thereby maximizing space.

Temperature Place a thermometer in the shade near the centre of your greenhouse and then check the temperature at different times of the day during sunny and cooler weather against the optimum temperature that your plants require and compensate if necessary by ventilating. The temperature readings you record should be used to determine what plants you can grow and when.

Many greenhouses are fitted with vent openers that open automatically when the greenhouse reaches a certain temperature. This is a really useful feature and avoids the concern about whether or not your plants are achieving adequate ventilation.

Plants will dry out very quickly in the greenhouse; water in the morning rather than in the evening.

Ventilation Space your plants evenly around the greenhouse so that the air is evenly distributed. Greenhouses can be prone to overheating in very hot weather and need as much help with ventilation as possible. Choose a ventilation system appropriate to the site, size and design of your greenhouse.

Try opening the doors in the morning depending on the weather and leave them open until late afternoon. This will protect the plants from frost at night, but will keep the greenhouse cool during the day.

In hot weather, water down the greenhouse path in order to cool the entire unit down quickly.

Soil Commercial potting compost is fine for use in the kitchen garden greenhouse. If possible, choose a compost that is specially designed for containers or seedlings.

Maintenance At the beginning of the season, clean and disinfect the greenhouse, using an eco-friendly disinfectant if possible. In between disinfecting, spray the walls and corners of the greenhouse with a jet hose to help prevent spider mites and whitefly.

Keep the greenhouse in good order by tidying up as soon as you've made a mess. Remove any cuttings or trimmings that have been taken from tomatoes or other plants.

On particularly hot or dry days, plants may need some shading, which can be achieved by spreading fabric or screens on the sunny side of the greenhouse.

In the winter, the greenhouse can be insulated by using bubblewrap attached to the sides

BELOW: *Place your greenhouse in a convenient sunny site, near a water tap, and allow for adequate space inside to move around.*

Polytunnel practicalities

These are a type of greenhouse and come in many sizes. Made of polythene and supported by galvanized steel hoops, they're easy and quick to erect and last for around five years. The hoops should be no more than 75 cm (2½ ft) apart. If spaced further apart, the sheeting will droop over the plants and potentially damage them.

A major advantage of a polytunnel is cost. For a similar amount you can buy a polytunnel four or five times bigger than a small, good-quality greenhouse and therefore grow many more crops.

Polytunnels are not as permanent as greenhouses, but have the advantage of being quite easy to move around the garden, thereby avoiding the problem of building up disease from growing the same crop for a few years in the same place (see Crop Rotation, page 16).

Cold frames and hot beds

A cold frame is an efficient, less expensive substitute for a greenhouse and can be portable. Cold frames have a box structure with solid or glass sides and a sloping lid that opens to provide ventilation. They offer a good way of acclimatizing plants to the outside world before planting outdoors in vegetable beds.

Site the cold frame near the greenhouse if possible to avoid carrying the plants far and also to benefit from some of the reflected warmth from the greenhouse. Alternatively, place near the veg beds to make it convenient when transferring plants. The frame should be aligned so that its sloping lid receives maximum sunlight and heat.

BELOW LEFT: Polytunnels are a popular alternative to greenhouses. They have the same function, but are less permanent and can be moved around the garden.

BELOW: Cold frames are handy glass boxes, great for acclimatizing young plants before transferring them outside.

A hot bed is the same as a cold frame but insulated, usually with straw, old carpet, bubble wrap or matting, and then placed on top of a pit or bed of fresh manure. When the manure breaks down, it releases heat within the frame and produces a hot microclimate. The fresh manure needs to be buried as soon as possible after collection, as it loses heat when uncovered.

You can buy ready-made cold frames or hot beds, but they can also be constructed using wood and plastic sheeting.

Cloches and fleece

A cloche is a very useful device for vegetable beds. Placed over the soil in the spring, cloches will warm it up ready for planting seeds and seedlings, protect young plants from the wind and frost and are an excellent way of acclimatizing the seedlings to the outdoors after transferring them from the greenhouse. They are usually used either at the beginning or end of the growing season to extend it by protecting tender, young plants.

They come in all different sizes and can be long enough to cover whole rows, or try bell cloches that can be popped over individual plants. At the end of each season, clean cloches by washing in water and a little washing-up liquid, removing the algae that has built up.

Used in the same way as cloches and often referred to as 'floating cloches', fleece is a finely woven material that allows the water and air to penetrate. It can be draped over bended wires pushed into the soil and attached with some clips or bricks to keep plants protected from frost or from pests such as carrot fly or the cabbage white butterfly. It is less suitable for windy sites, as it can easily tear.

RIGHT: Cloches are very useful to place over young plants and seedlings to give them a head start.

BELOW RIGHT: Bell cloches are ideal for popping over the top of individual plants.

BELOW: A fleece tunnel will protect against unwelcome pests and allow plenty of ventilation.

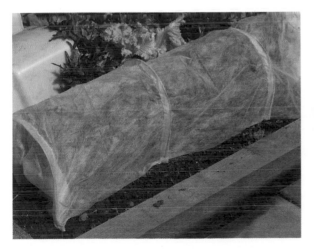

SOWING AND PLANTING
The seeds of success

Before you start planning your crops, you'll need to decide whether you're going to grow them from seed or if you're going to buy them as plug plants. Some seeds need to be nurtured under cover in seed trays or pots, while others can be planted directly outside and then the seedlings thinned out. It's therefore best to check the individual requirements for each plant type before deciding which ones to grow (see pages 64–139), and in relation to how much space you have and the growing conditions available to you.

Buying seeds and plug plants

Seeds are easily available and can be bought at many different outlets, from small hardware shops and supermarkets to garden centres and specialist nurseries. Seed catalogues probably offer the widest variety of seeds and can be ordered very easily either by mail order or online. If possible, buy organic seeds.

Plant plugs are young seedlings that can be bought from garden centres or nurseries, or by mail order or online and delivered by mail. Plant them as soon as possible after you've brought them home or received them and plant outside as you would home-raised seedlings (see below).

Growing from seed

Seeds need warmth, moisture and soil to germinate. Some plants will take longer than others to germinate depending on when you plant them and how warm it is. It's always best to sow more seeds than you need, as some may not germinate.

LEFT: Seedlings are your babies – handle with care.

Sowing seeds outside

Before sowing seeds outside, you'll need to break up any hard clumps of soil to loosen the ground. When you plant will depend on your climate. The outdoor temperature must be right for germination, so check on the seed packet when the optimum time is for sowing. If necessary, warm the soil first by covering with a cloche or fleece for a few days beforehand.

Wild birds and your chickens will be keeping an eye out on where you have planted seeds, so protect them with fencing or netting until established.

1 Prepare a seedbed by breaking down the soil and raking it over to create a smooth surface where the soil is fine and crumbly. Remove any stones, hard lumps of earth or twigs.

2 Push soil through a soil sieve to give it a fine texture and to remove any stones.

3 Using a garden line, mark out your row. Use the edge of a hoe, a rake or a broom handle to make a seed drill in the surface of the soil deep enough to plant the seed, but not so deep that the seed will be covered by too much soil, otherwise the seedling won't be able to reach the surface. It's best to follow the growing instructions specific to the plant (see pages 64–139).

4 Water the drill and place the seed according to the plant's specific growing instructions (see pages 64–139). Draw back the soil gently over the seeds with a rake or hoe.

5 Gently firm down the soil with the back of the rake or your hands, but not so firm that you compact the soil. If your soil has a tendency to compact after rain or watering, cover the seeds with potting compost instead of soil. Water in along the row using a fine-spray rose on a watering can.

Sowing seeds indoors

If you have a greenhouse, polytunnel or cold frame, you can sow seeds under cover early so that the seedlings are ready to plant out once the soil is warm enough. If not, you can use a windowsill indoors. They can be sown in a variety of different containers, such as small pots and cell trays. When using the latter, don't be tempted to put too many seeds in one cell, otherwise they will be fighting for root space and some may not thrive.

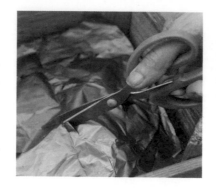

1 If using a wooden box, line the base with polythene to prevent the wood from rotting and cut holes in the polythene base for drainage. If using a plastic ready-made tray, make sure that it's throughly clean before use. Fill the seed tray with compost.

2 Use a good-quality seed compost and break up any lumps – if possible, pass the compost through a soil sieve. Fill the tray with compost until it's overflowing and tap the tray to settle the compost. Wipe off the excess compost so that the seed tray is full.

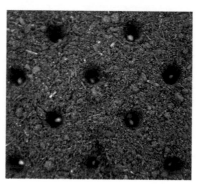

3 Firm the compost with your hand or with a firming tool (a moulded piece of plastic that creates holes for planting) until the surface sits just below the top of the seed tray.

4 Open the seed packet, take a pinch of seeds and gently sprinkle them over the soil. If you've used a firming tool that has spikes for creating holes, drop the seeds into the holes.

5 Cover with a fine scattering of compost, depending on the instructions on the seed packet, as not all seeds need covering. Water the seed tray so that the compost is moist but not waterlogged.

Label using indelible ink, putting the date on one side of the label and the name of the plant on the other. Put the seed tray in a suitable position. Different seeds need different conditions – again, check the seed packet for instructions – but they usually require somewhere warm and sunny, such as a greenhouse or a windowsill. Keep the seeds moist by watering as necessary.

Transplanting seedlings

Some plants can be grown directly in their final growing space, particularly those that don't like their roots being disturbed, such as root crops, but many will benefit by being grown first in pots or in a seedbed and then transplanted, especially if you are moving them from indoors to outdoors.

When seedlings have germinated and reached through the soil, make sure that they're big enough to handle before you transplant them or thin them out. Follow the recommended instructions for each type of plant. Wait until all frosts have passed before transplanting most seedlings from indoors to outdoors, and don't leave them until the leaves have turned yellow or too big. Water seedlings before transplanting or thinning to minimize the shock and give them the best chance of recovery.

Try to choose a dull day to transplant when the ground is moist. Harden the plants off by bringing them from indoors in their cell trays or containers to the outside for a few days to get them used to their new environment. Prepare the area where they're going to be planted by lightly forking up the soil and removing weeds. Rake in some well-rotted compost or add a base dressing of fertilizer.

how to transplant

Wait until seedlings are big enough to handle before you transplant them. A rule of thumb is to wait until two or three leaves have grown, but some may need more.

1 Ease out the seedling very gently and keep handling to a minimum. This can be done by simply loosening up the soil with a dibber, the end of a pencil, a knitting needle or any other small, stick-like object. Try to lift the seedling by the leaves and avoid touching the roots. If transplanting from pots, tap the side and gently tip the pot so that the seedling falls onto the soil.

2 Dig a hole big enough to accommodate the root ball of each seedling with the lowest leaves just above the surface level and place the seedlings in the holes. This is best done using a trowel. If planting in drills, space each seedling at the required distance apart (see individual vegetable entries in Chapter 3) using a measuring stick for accurate spacing. It's useful to line up each seedling in place along the drill first and then plant each one individually.

3 When planting, hold the plant with one hand and push the soil around the plant so that it remains firm and is supported by the soil. Top up the soil so that the lowest leaves are just above the surface level. Water in and mulch (see page 57) when you've finished planting each row.

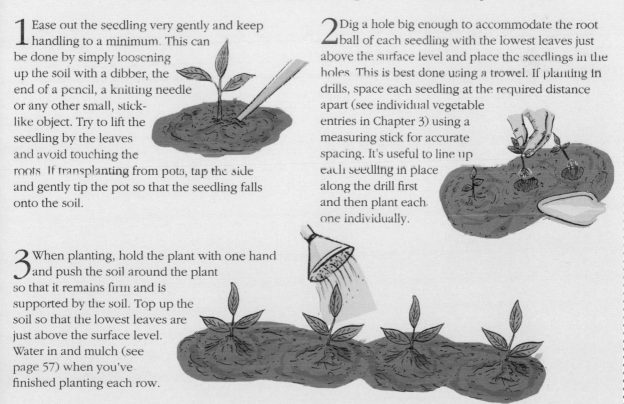

Thinning

Seedlings usually need thinning out in order to give each one space to grow and thrive. This is often necessary when they're grown in cell trays or in rows that have become overcrowded. If left as they are, the seedlings will have to fight for root space and nutrients in the compost and as a consequence will fail to grow properly, turn pale in colour and possibly die.

We usually plant more seeds than we need and most seed packets contain far more seeds than you'll need for your plot. The time to thin out is when the leaves start to touch each other and have sprouted their second set of leaves. If left too long, they will become weak and limp.

Dispose of the thinnings by composting them (see pages 24–27) – if you leave them at the side of the rows, slugs and snails will make a meal of them, possibly along with all your growing seedlings too.

Thinning is also known as pricking out.

Wait until the seedlings have all emerged and pinch out any surplus plants at the soil level. Repeat this process whenever they are looking too crowded. Begin by leaving each plant clear of the others and then progressively remove seedlings until you have them planted at the required distance apart, depending on the plant type (see pages 64–139).

LEFT AND RIGHT: Radish seedlings emerge very quickly and do not like to be overcrowded. Thin the smaller or weaker plants (left) and leave the stronger ones (right) to grow, keeping them weed free.

Tip: Rather than discarding them on the compost heap, thinnings of salad leaves or herbs such as basil are wonderful for using in salads or for flavouring pasta dishes.

thinning out fine seedlings

*Basil grows well if thinned into small clumps, which are
then put into individual pots to grow.*

1 Choose the strongest-looking
seedlings with the biggest root
system. Simply loosen the soil of
the seedling and ease it out.

2 Carefully divide up the
seedlings into separate plants.

3 Make a hole big enough for
the roots of each seedling and
transplant into its own space.

4 Gently firm the soil around
the seedlings and water in
afterwards in case any roots have
become loose.

Care plan for young plants

When young seedlings are first planted in the ground, they will need a little tender loving care, so follow these simple guidelines to give them the best start.

Treat the plants very gently and prepare the soil for them before you transplant them.

If transferring from indoors to outdoors, harden them off beforehand by bringing them outside for a few days. Start off by leaving them out during the day and putting them back indoors overnight, then a few days later leave them out the entire time before planting them in the ground.

Protect seedlings for the first few days from hot sun by placing an upturned flowerpot over the top. You can also use sheets of newspapers to protect plants from the hot sun if there is no wind. Use a cloche or cover with fleece at night if the temperature has a tendency to fall steeply (see page 41).

Protect young plants from pests until they've had the chance to establish, keeping an eye out for slug, snail or caterpillar attacks. Fleece offers good protection while plants are still tender.

The tender young plants make delicious snacks for your hens, garden birds, rabbits and even squirrels. If you experience this problem, cover young plants with netting and use as many deterrents as are available to you.

Young plants shouldn't have to compete with weeds for nutrients in the soil, so keep weeds down by hoeing or weeding by hand.

Young plants can be mulched. This will help retain soil heat and moisture, reduce water evaporation, keep the weeds down and provide protection against the wind. Try mulching with grass clippings or leaf mould placed gently around the base of the seedling.

Don't feed seedlings when they are first transplanted, as this decreases their ability to withstand the weather.

Water well each day using the fine rose on a watering can until the seedlings have become established (a jet of water from a hose will be too strong). Seedlings have a delicate root system while they are still small and can easily dry out in warm weather.

Tip: The cardboard tubes found inside rolls of kitchen paper and toilet paper make ideal containers for young plants that don't like their roots to be disturbed when the time comes to plant them out.

Cut the longer tubes into short lengths, place in a seed tray and fill with soil or compost, then plant with seeds. When the seedlings have grown to a suitable size, simply plant the entire pot in the ground and in time the cardboard tube will biodegrade without causing any damage to the new, tender roots.

making newspaper pots

Newspaper pots are an excellent way of making biodegradable seed pots for little expense. You simply plant your seeds and wait for the seedlings to emerge. When the seedlings are ready to be planted out, dig a hole in the soil and plant the newspaper pot with the seedling straight into the ground. This will give the least disturbance to the plants roots and the newspaper will biodegrade into the soil. It's also an excellent way of recycling newspaper. Using a paper potter bought from the garden centre is ideal as they make perfect little pots, but you can also use a straight-sided glass and push the bottom onto a firm surface to secure the base.

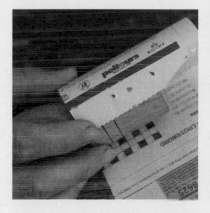  

1 Cut dry newspapers into strips approximately 8 x 57 cm (3 x 22 in) Take one strip and roll it loosely around the potter.

2 Fold over the excess paper neatly at the base, making sure that there are no gaps.

3 Press the potter firmly onto the wooden base.

4 Remove the pot and fill with compost, ready for planting your seeds.

Natural fertilizers

Plants can eventually use up many of the valuable nutrients in the soil, becoming impoverished and in need of additional replenishment. Natural fertilizers such as nettles and comfrey are excellent resources that many people will find already growing in their garden.

Not-so-nasty nettles

These plants are often seen as the bad boys of the garden. They sting, take over any spare bit of garden and grow just about anywhere. I hated nettles for quite some time, having rolled down a steep hill of nettles at the age of five, and I still remember the throbbing pain. But now, as a kitchen gardener, I'm a convert. Nettles are great for the garden; the stinging nettle is one of the most important native plants for wildlife, supporting many different species of insect including some of the most colourful butterflies. They can also be made into great-tasting soups and therapeutic teas.

Nettles are full of nutrients that will help your vegetable plants to grow, so take advantage of their wonderful benefits by making them into a free, organic and entirely safe liquid feed. Feed to your plants weekly and watch them thrive.

An organic liquid treat

1 Wearing thick gardening gloves, collect a large bunch of fresh nettles – preferably young ones, as they will compost more quickly, but any nettles will do.

2 The nettles are best bruised, so cut up with scissors or, even better, tear them into pieces and scrunch them up. Put the nettles into a bucket with a lid and cover them with water.

3 Place a brick or other weight on top of the nettles and then cover the bucket with the lid.

Leave the liquid to brew for three to four weeks. It can become rather smelly, so place the bucket somewhere out of the way and where it can be left undisturbed.

Once the nettle feed is ready, dilute it until it's the colour of tea – approximately 1 part nettle feed to 10 parts water. Water plants well with the solution. Continue to top the bucket up with nettles to provide a liquid feed all summer. At the end of the season, throw the nettle sludge onto the compost heap and rinse the bucket well, ready for use the following season.

GROWING IN CONTAINERS

If you have limited space in your garden, there is still an abundance of produce you can grow in containers. Many urbanites can grow vegetables using the smallest of balcony or patio as well as indoor windowsills. They can also be highly decorative – all sorts of colours and sizes of pots are available, along with eye-catching mulches to place on top of the compost such as broken shells, broken china or glass beads.

Pots with plenty

Clay and terracotta These come in many different sizes and designs. When buying, make sure that they are frost-proof rather than frost-resistant to avoid them developing cracks during hard winters. If you stand the pots on 'feet', there will be less risk of frost damage. Terracotta and clay pots also have a tendency to dry out quicker; line the inside with polythene to help contain moisture.

Metal containers These give a more contemporary look, or you can pick up old galvanized jugs and buckets in a junk shop or market for a rustic or vintage effect. They have fewer tendencies to dry out, although they conduct the heat and cold more readily.

Wooden containers Old fruit boxes, window boxes or wooden tubs are very attractive. If the fruit boxes have gaps in the sides, line them first with polythene (try using an old, cut-up compost bag or a bin liner), cutting holes in the bottom for drainage before filling up with compost.

RIGHT: Growing vegetables and herbs in a variety of containers is an effective and attractive way of gardening in a small space.

Plastic containers These are light, making them easy to move, and practical, being less prone to drying out than terracotta and unaffected by frost. Look out for attractive plastic pots that imitate terracotta convincingly.

Hanging baskets Some plants grow very well in hanging baskets, such as herbs or tumbling

tomatoes. Strawberries also love hanging baskets – they make for very easy picking and keep the fruit above ground level away from raiding pests such as mice or squirrels.

Other containers Look for any recycled materials that you may have around the house; old tins, buckets and kettles all work well. Make drainage holes in the bottom, and if they are to sit inside on a windowsill, place them in a tray to catch the water as it drains out of the bottom.

Size When choosing a container, make sure that it's the right size for the type of plant you're going to grow. Root vegetables will need deep pots, while salads, spinach and beetroot work well in shallow pots, as the roots sit near the top. Tomatoes or courgettes need larger pots to accommodate their roots and will also possibly require cane supports, depending on the variety you choose.

Drainage Most plants need good drainage and don't like to be waterlogged. If your containers haven't already got drainage holes in the base, you'll need to drill some. Place broken pieces of stone, old crocks or a broken-up old polystyrene planter in the base of the containers before filling with a compost that offers good drainage.

Watering Plants in containers tend to dry out more easily and will therefore need regular checking for moisture. A windowsill acts as a mini greenhouse for growing plants and so moisture levels will need checking very frequently.

Bear in mind that if your pots are kept on a paved patio, the stone or bricks will absorb heat during the day and be released at night, so the plants are likely to be in a warmer environment than if planted in the ground.

Don't rely on rainfall to keep the plants adequately watered, as the rain will often not penetrate the leaves or be heavy enough to penetrate down to the roots. There are water-retaining gels or powders that can be mixed with the compost when planting up your containers, which swell up when wet and then release water gradually back into the compost. Decorative mulches or gravel can also be placed on the surface of the compost, which will help retain moisture. Smaller pots will dry out more quickly than larger pots.

Compost Use a soil- or loam-based compost when growing vegetables. Most multi-purpose composts are suitable for using in containers.

Because of the relatively small amount of compost available in pots, the plant will be able to draw only a limited amount of nutrients, so it's advisable to feed your container plants regularly with a controlled-release fertilizer or a general-purpose plant food.

Position Most vegetables like full sun and as much light as possible. Choose your positioning carefully, as the pots will be difficult to move about and heavy once they are full of compost and water. If you are growing any tall climbing plants, avoid a windy position. Make sure that the pots are placed near an outside tap for easy watering.

Tip: To make an eye-catching display with your containers of produce, rather than just growing green-leaved plants, choose from the many different coloured-leaf varieties available. For example, try growing purple basil, chard stems in waves of bright pinks, purples and oranges or radicchio leaves with their deep-red veins.

OPPOSITE: *Save vintage wooden boxes, galvanized buckets, baskets or trays to make a collection of containers for vegetable growing.*

WATERING
The life-support system

To be able to run a successful garden farm with vegetables and hens or other animals, you must have water. Since there is no need to use drinking water to water your plants, catching rainwater is the most economical and ecological way to hydrate the garden. Don't waste water – it's the Earth's invaluable asset and should be treated with great respect, so think carefully about whether you really need to water your lawn when the precious water you've saved can be put to more productive use.

When to water

It's far better to water deeply and less often than to water a little but more frequently. A rule of thumb is to make sure that your garden receives at least 2.5 cm (1 in) of water weekly. Plant a small pot or cup near your vegetables as an indicator of your natural rainwater levels.

When watering, don't just sprinkle a little water aimlessly around, which will often only lead to it evaporating and won't give the soil any real benefit. Instead, water deeply and regularly in sections. If the weather is hot and dry and your plants wilt during the afternoon, this doesn't necessarily mean that they need water and they may regain their balance overnight. But if plants are wilting early in the morning, water them immediately.

Don't think that just because the ground looks dry it needs watering. Test by pushing your finger down into the soil and feel whether it's damp underneath the surface, or use a trowel to make a small hole. If the ground is dry below around 5–10 cm (2–4 in), it needs watering.

Watering plants is best done in the morning or last thing in the evening. Slugs prefer a moist soil and do most of their damage at night, so watering in the morning is preferable. Watering in the middle of the day when it's hot and sunny will not only waste water due to rapid evaporation but hot sun on wet plants can damage leaves and fruit. Bear in mind that watering takes time, so make sure that you set enough aside to care for and nurture all of your garden plants and animals. Remember that you'll need to water even if it has been raining, as rain often fails to soak the ground down to the roots of plants and sometimes just sits on the soil surface before evaporating.

Soil type also affects water absorption. Clay soils retain water well in summer but drain badly in winter, sandy soils function in reverse and loamy soils are well balanced, retaining moisture in summer yet draining adequately in winter.

Watering needs

Each individual type of plant has varying watering needs and at different times during their development. Some prefer the soil to be continually moist, while others prefer a dry soil and need little water or, as in the case of cucurbits,

hate water on their leaves. Always check the watering requirements for each type of plant (see pages 64–139), as it's very easy to kill a plant off with too much or too little water.

Look after your hens, particularly in hot summer months or freezing cold winter months. They must have fresh water every day. In the winter, you'll especially need to check that their water doesn't freeze up once or twice daily, and in the summer they will need extra water.

Water resources

Mains water This is the easiest yet most expensive option. If it's impossible for you to avoid using mains water, use it carefully and try to

ABOVE: Galvanized watering cans will last longer, but plastic cans are lighter.

ABOVE RIGHT: Water butts collect rainwater from guttering and can easily be disguised and hidden by shrubs or vines.

cut costs by backing it up with other options. Make sure that you have an outside tap near to the vegetable patch and hen-keeping area – there's nothing worse than having to carry heavy watering cans and buckets of water around in the depths of winter. Also ensure that pipes are well insulated so that the water supply doesn't freeze up or burst a pipe.

Rainwater Water butts used to collect rainwater via the guttering from your house or sheds are an asset for any garden, providing you with an invaluable, natural and free water supply. They were traditionally made of wood, but you can now buy relatively cheap plastic butts in an array of shapes and sizes. Place them in as many areas as you can and set up guttering on all your sheds that connects to the water butt. You can also buy connecting pipes that form a chain from one butt to the other. I'm always amazed by how quickly they fill up following a downpour. When setting up the water butts, place them on bricks or concrete blocks so that the taps are high enough for a watering can or bucket to fit underneath.

Old tin baths, plastic dustbins, fruit barrels or cleaned oil drums are useful alternatives to purpose-designed water butts, but make sure that you cover them with lids to avoid evaporation.

Grey water This is water that comes from household baths, showers or the kitchen and its use in the garden makes good ecological sense, but it must be free from bleach, chemicals and oil, and contain a minimal amount of soap or detergents. Grey water can go 'off', so use it as soon as possible. Don't use grey water to give to your hens – they must have fresh water.

Rivers, lakes, streams and ponds If you are fortunate enough to have a river, lake, stream or pond on your land, it's advisable to ask for a water test from your local authority before using it on your vegetable plot to check that it's free from contamination. Ponds are relatively easy to construct or install, attract abundant wildlife and are another valuable water asset.

How to water

Watering cans This is the preferable way of watering, as you can target each plant according to its needs and water is least wasted. Watering cans come in all different shapes, sizes and materials. Choose a large, good-quality one – plastic cans are lighter than galvanized – with different grades of rose. A fine rose is essential for watering seeds and seedlings; turn the rose upwards so that it doesn't damage fragile leaves.

Hosepipes It is usual practice to attach a hose to the mains tap in the garden. Choose a good-quality hose, as they invariably have to withstand a fair amount of hauling and dragging around the garden, and buy a fitting that offers several different varieties of spray, including a mist spray and fine spray for watering seeds and seedlings. Don't underestimate the length of hosepipe you will need – it's very frustrating if the hose won't quite reach to your furthest vegetable beds.

Many water companies impose a hosepipe ban in certain areas in the summer, which can be a gardener's nightmare. Millions of gallons of water

LEFT: Water each plant according to its individual needs and buy a good-quality attachment for your hose (ideally a spray or nozzle where you can change the intensity of the water jet).

go to waste each year through leaks from the water companies, so make sure that you don't add to this wastage by always remembering to switch off the tap of the hose after you've watered.

Soaker hoses These are hoses that are pierced along their length with lots of holes and can be buried below the ground along the beds to direct water straight to the target. They also cut down on evaporation.

Sprinklers These are very easy to use and will water over a wide area, but can waste water by failing to target the water effectively. So if you decide to use this method, you will need to group together plants that have the same water requirements when planting. Always use sprinklers when there is little wind to avoid water being blown off course.

There are several types of sprinkler on the market. Fixed sprinklers will often have a dial that changes the spray pattern, but they can be light and tend to move around through the pressure of the water being sprayed out. Rotating sprinklers are effective, but have a habit of tipping over. Pulsating sprinklers are usually more reliable, can be controlled to throw the water at a distance and last longer.

Ways of conserving moisure

Mulch This is organic material used to cover the surface of the soil to prevent it drying out. Natural mulches include straw, grass clippings, leaf mould, bark clippings, coffee grains and tea bags/leaves.

Organic matter This acts as a sponge in the soil. Prepare the soil before planting (see pages 20–23) and dig in plenty of organic matter, which will conserve valuable water and feed the soil. Organic matter comes from well-rotted manure, garden compost, straw or anything that will rot down and hold water.

Wind breaks If you live in a windy area, think about using these to prevent the wind causing evaporation. They can be natural barriers, such as trees, shrubs or hedges, or wooden fences.

Hoeing Regular hoeing not only keeps down the weeds but opens the surface of the soil so that the water can penetrate to the roots.

BELOW: *Weeds can steal valuable nutrients and moisture away from plants. Weed your beds often by hand or hoe.*

Tip: Bury a flowerpot in the soil next to the plant that needs targeting. If you fill the flowerpot instead of watering the plant directly, it will get the water it requires without disturbing the roots.

PESTS AND DISEASES
Winning the battle

Most gardeners will have to tackle pests and diseases in the
kitchen garden, some being easier than others to manage. The
trick is to make the garden function as biodynamically as possible
as a natural way of combating the problems that can affect your veg.
Don't expect total elimination of pests and diseases – their occurrence is a
natural part of plant life. Aim for low plant losses rather than no losses at all.

Natural defences

Without resorting to chemicals, rotating the crops
in your vegetables beds (see page 16) will keep
the soil healthy and attract beneficial wildlife into
your garden. If you use chemical solutions to treat
pests, remember that the chemicals will kill all the
living things on your plants, not just the
unwelcome ones.

Where possible, buy disease-resistant plant
varieties. All plants, however, have their own
mechanisms for coping with pests and diseases.
By keeping yours well watered and nourished to
make them strong and healthy, they will be better
able to defend themselves against attacks than if
undernourished or weak.

Make your garden environment as hostile as
you can for the pests by removing weeds and any
other potential hiding areas and creating barriers
using netting, mesh and fleece. Also, try
companion planting as another natural form of
defence (see pages 17–19).

Pest control measures

Slugs and snails These are probably your
worst enemies in the kitchen garden, devouring
young plants if given half the chance. Slug pellets
are available, but most are not organic. There are
organic deterrents, such as the naturally occurring
fertilizer iron (ferric) phosphate. Other organic
methods include the following:

Beer traps Slugs and snails are attracted to the
smell of yeast and beer traps are designed to
attract the slugs to the beer instead of the plants,
but they're not always effective at gathering up all
the slugs in the garden and you're bound to lose
some of your crops. The traps will need to be
emptied and refilled every two or three days.
Don't put slugs and snails into the compost or they
will rot and make the compost smell bad.

To make your own beer trap

1 Fill a shallow pan or plastic food container
with 2.5–5 cm (1–2 in) of cheap beer (there
is reputedly more yeast in draught beer than
bottled beer, but any sort will do).

2 Bury the container so that the lip is at about
ground level, enabling the slugs and snails to
crawl into the trap with ease.

3 Suspend a cover over the trap that protects the
beer but allows slugs and snails to enter.

Broken eggshells/sharp grit Difficult for slugs and snails to cross, so place a layer around each plant.

Manual removal Picking snails, slugs and caterpillars off by hand can feel like a thankless task, but it's effective and they can be dispatched quickly and efficiently by putting them in a jar of brine.

Rabbits These creatures will happily nibble away all day and night at your vegetables. The best defence is to install a boundary fence.

Squirrels and mice Fruit is very attractive to squirrels and mice, and as soon as a strawberry is just at its ripest, they will home in on it. Try putting netting around the most vulnerable plants, but squirrels are good at breaking in. Achieving an effective deterrent will be a matter of trial and error.

Moles Humane mole traps are available as a way of catching these creatures, which will burrow their way through the veg patch and create havoc.

Hens I have a particularly rebellious hen who constantly escapes and makes Houdini look like an amateur. She seems to know when I've planted out especially tasty spinach or salad leaves and will eat the whole row before I've got to her, though she always takes the green shoots and leaves the red ones. During the growing season, try to contain hens if you can and don't let them range freely over your vegetables.

Cats Excellent at keeping away unwanted rodents, but also partial to using a bit of loose soil as a toilet, causing damage by digging up seedbeds and the soil in containers. Cats also hunt and will take any useful predators such as small birds, frogs and toads. Even if you do not have a cat, chances are that you'll be visited by a neighbour's cat. Keeping a dog will deter them, or there is an electronic device that uses infra-red to detect movement and then emits a sound outside the range of human hearing yet intolerable to a cat. It does them no harm, and they learn to avoid the area. For your own cat, there is no known solution other than perhaps using a water pistol and keeping a 24-hour watch. Sprinkling pepper dust around the plants is also a possible deterrent.

Dogs Dogs are more trainable than cats and you can usually teach them not to step over the line of the vegetable area (except when they're chasing the cats).

Children It's a real pleasure to introduce children to the garden farm, but make sure they don't trample on or pull up your vegetables. If you teach them a healthy respect of the garden and involve them in planting, watering and nurturing, they will take as much care of the garden as you do.

RIGHT: Hens will always be on the lookout for tasty young leaves to nibble on.

Combating diseases

These are often more difficult to deal with because at their onset they're less visible. They can slowly creep up on you, and before you've noticed and had a chance to treat them, they've taken a hold. Diseases can survive for years in the soil while they wait dormant for a new plant.

In addition to choosing disease-resistant plant varieties wherever possible, good cultivation is required to encourage healthy growth, together with some basic garden hygiene measures. Avoid drought stress and under- or overfeeding. Space your plants well, as overcrowding can lead to an epidemic of disease. Clear away and destroy old or damaged leaves (don't add to the compost heap). Inspect plants regularly for early signs of disease and treat promptly.

PEST	DESCRIPTION	DAMAGE	TREATMENT
Aphids	Black, green, grey or white. Tiny and some can fly.	Weaken plants and prevent growth. Cause foliage to curl.	* Encourage insect or bird predators. * Spray with insecticidal soap. * Spray with clean water. * Attract ladybirds, lacewings and hoverflies whose larvae devour aphids.
Caterpillars and grubs	Larvae of butterlies, moths, etc. Some live or hibernate in soil and others are more visible.	Feed on leaves, fruits, roots and stems.	* Pick off and dispatch; check underside of leaves. * Spray with a solution of 60 g (2¼ oz) salt in 4.5 litres (1 gallon) water. * Rake soil to expose for birds to destroy.
Slugs and snails	Molluscs that feed on young plants, mostly at night in damp conditions.	Eat leaves and shoots.	* Hand pick if possible at dusk and when weather is damp and wet check underside of leaves. * Use beer traps (see page 58) and barriers of grit. * Attract natural predators such as toads.
Red spider mite	Tiny, sap-sucking insects that live in warm, dry environments.	Yellow spotted leaves and fine webs.	* Keep plants moist. * Mist the foliage, particularly in greenhouses. * Spray with insecticidal soap.

DISEASES	DESCRIPTION AND DAMAGE	TREATMENT
Canker	Creates lesions and bark and tissue death on fruit trees and woody plants.	* Prune affected shoots. * Avoid susceptible varieties.
Club root	Particularly affects cabbages and other brassicas. Infection of the root prevalent in some soils, particularly active in warm, wet soil. Roots become distorted and growth prevented.	* Prevention is best. Limy soil reduces infection. * Start plants off in sterile compost and establish before planting out. * Place a collar around the base of the stem to protect young plants.
Mildews	These are parasitic fungi, either downy or powdery mildew. Look for a powdery grey dust covering distorted foliage. Downy mildew produces yellow areas and a grey, fuzzy patch underneath the leaves.	* Can be caused by overcrowding and dry conditions. * Mulch and water well during dry spells. * Downy mildew occurs in damp or humid conditions, sometimes late in the season. Avoid overcrowding and water during the morning. * Pinch off infected shoots and leaves * Grow resistant varieties.
Rot	Fungi and bacteria that cause decay of plant tissues. Occurs in damp or waterlogged conditions.	* Ensure adequate air circulation and good drainage. * Avoid overwatering and overcrowding. * Destroy infected plants immediately.
Rusts	Fungal disease that produces tiny dark spots on stems and leaves with red or brown spore bearing pustules. Rusts tend to disfigure the plant rather than destroy it.	* Clear infected leaves to avoid contamination. * Sterilize tools and plant same stock in a different position next season.
Scabs	Fungal and bacterial diseases causing crusty patches on leaves, roots, fruits and twigs.	* Avoid over-liming. Water, manure, mulch regularly. * Clear affected leaves and shoots in autumn. * Don't store affected fruits and roots – eat immediately.
Viruses	Common on a range of plants. Look for yellow spotted, scrunched-up leaves, stunted growth or poor yields. Viruses are usually spread by pests or contact with hands/tools.	* Grow plants that are certified virus free. * Wash tools and hands regularly to avoid transmission. * Destroy affected plants. * Don't compost infected plants.
Wilt	Some plants will completely collapse, usually from the effects of poor drainage, overwatering or cold, wet weather.	* Avoid overwatering. * When plants have collapsed, it's usually too late to save them.

CHAPTER THREE

The Kitchen Garden

The kitchen garden will be the hub of your garden farm. Given the abundance of different types of vegetables, fruits and herbs, it's very important to choose your crops carefully. For example, in my house everyone hates aubergines, so we don't grow them, but we love courgettes and beetroot, and just can't get enough of them. Don't use valuable growing space on something that doesn't work well for you or your family. Excess vegetables are always useful for bartering with friends, or, if you have a like-minded neighbour, try sharing your produce – say, you grow enough courgettes for both of you and they grow the spinach.

Vegetables, fruits and herbs have such a lot of individual varieties, and although here I've recommended certain ones for each type of produce, the end results are still largely down to trial and error. Some varieties will work best in your particular soil and climate and others have been produced that are disease resistant. It will also depend on which seeds are available, either from your local garden centre or from a seed catalogue. My advice for novice gardeners is not to get too bogged down and confused by varieties. Simply choose something with the shape and colour that you recognize, then move on to experimenting in subsequent years.

Remember to always label your rows of plants or seed trays, and if you've kept a garden journal of what you've planted and where, take time to assess which varieties have worked well for you, so that next year you can either choose the same variety or try another one to improve your results. Documenting your planting is also very useful when it comes to crop rotation.

ROOT VEGETABLES

Root vegetables often form the basis of kitchen cuisine. No kitchen garden should be without potatoes or carrots, and the deep-red veins that run through beetroot leaves are just the temptress for what grows beneath the surface.

Potatoes

High in vitamin C and potassium, potatoes are one of the most popular vegetables. In the UK and the USA, the average adult eats around 60 kg (132 lb) of potatoes a year. They are easy to grow and come in a wide range of varieties, from the large baking potato to small, nut-like salad potatoes. If you grow several crops, you can have a constant supply of potatoes throughout the season.

Earlies provide 'new' potatoes in the summer, the first earlies being ready to harvest within three months and the second earlies taking just a few weeks longer. Maincrop potatoes are ideal for storing over the winter and tend to be larger. Plant first earlies before planting maincrop and second earlies, but choose just early varieties if you have limited space.

Potatoes are only half-hardy; the young leaves will be killed by late frosts in spring and the stems will be killed by early frosts in autumn.

The easiest way of growing potatoes is buying and then planting 'chitted' potatoes – small seed potatoes that have been induced to develop small shoots before planting. When planted, the stems and leaves will be produced above ground, while below ground the tubers swell and develop in summer or early autumn.

When buying seed potatoes, make sure they are certifiably free from viruses.

Best varieties *Anya AGM*: excellent salad potato with a nutty flavour; *Kestrel*: second early variety with good slug resistance; *Accent*: first early waxy new potato; *Maris Piper*: maincrop that produces excellent yields; *Desiree*: red-skinned, multi-purpose potato.

Growing site Light, sunny position. To avoid risk of soil contamination, don't grow potatoes on the same plot as the previous year.

Soil Deep, well-drained soil in a sunny position. Add plenty of well-rotted manure in the autumn of the previous year. Avoid waterlogged soil.

Planting Plant early to late spring.

Buy seed potatoes four to eight weeks before planting and set them with their 'eyes' upwards, either in egg boxes or seed trays. Place them in a light, cool position and wait for them to develop short, green shoots.

Before planting, rake up any large clots of soil. Dig a trench and plant each potato carefully so that you don't break off any of the shoots; plant upwards.

Tips If possible, warm the soil before planting by covering with cloches or black plastic a few weeks beforehand to accelerate growth. You can then either make holes and plant through the plastic or remove it before planting. You don't need to earth up potatoes that are grown in black plastic, as the plastic will protect the tubers from light (see opposite).

• Try watering in between the rows into the ridges to make a mini stream. This will seep through and give moisture underneath the potatoes without disturbing the soil on top.

As soon as they start to show through the ground, potatoes will need earthing up to protect them from the frost and the light. Break up the soil in between the rows with a fork or a hoe and draw up a pile of the loose soil against the stems to produce a ridge. Repeat this procedure every week during the growing season so that as the potatoes grow they don't reach the surface. If the potatoes are exposed to the light, they will become green and poisonous.

Spacing Plant earlies 15 cm (6 in) deep, 30 cm (12 in) apart with 60 cm (24 in) between rows; plant maincrop 40–75 cm (16–30 in) apart.

Germination Seed potatoes will take around 4–8 weeks to develop shoots.

Planting to harvesting Earlies: 13 weeks; maincrop: 22 weeks.

Pests and diseases *Potato blight*: brown, rust-like patches appear on the leaves or mould on the underside. Once this has taken hold there is nothing you can do other than to burn the plants and grow in another plot the next time. Try using a disease-resistant variety.

Slugs: these will burrow into the potato, creating grey holes. Avoid growing in wet soil.

Cyst eelworms: indicated by withered brown leaves and minute cysts on the roots. Avoid growing on the same plot and choose disease-resistant varieties.

Colorado beetle: this is uncommon, but if you have it you're required by law to notify the authorities.

Weeding Weed regularly by hand near the plant and hoe between rows.

Watering Water well in warm weather, particularly during the time when tubers are forming. Water liberally during early growth to encourage the tubers to swell and produce a heavy crop.

Harvesting Dig up earlies when the flowers open. Ease away the soil around the base of the stem to check if the potatoes are large enough and harvest on a dry day.

Lift maincrop in late summer if you're going to eat them immediately. Otherwise, leave in the ground and dig up as required, but there will be a greater chance of slug damage.

When lifting potatoes, be careful not to spike the potatoes with your garden fork. A potato fork is ideal, as it has flatter prongs that won't pierce the crop.

If potatoes are damp, expose them to the air for a few hours to dry them off.

Storing Store potatoes in a paper or hessian sack in a cool, dry place until required.

BELOW: *Forking up potatoes is like digging up hidden treasure from beneath the soil.*

Carrots

When growing carrots, you'll get used to the knobbly and odd-shaped examples that have been absent from supermarkets for many a year. When picked fresh and eaten raw, they are sweet and packed with flavour. They are such an adaptable vegetable and can be used in soups and stir-fries, and also make delicious, moist cakes.

Carrots are highly nutritious, rich in vitamin A and calcium, and a good source of fibre.

Tips   It's best to think carrots on a cool, rainy day, as the carrot fly can detect the scent of carrots better on a hot day or when the foliage is bruised.

• Sow carrots every three or four weeks for a constant supply from early spring to autumn.

Best varieties   Short-rooted – *Parmex*: round-rooted, great colour and good for planting in containers; medium-rooted – *Maincrop*: tasty and with a good resistance to carrot fly; long-rooted – *St Valery*: long and tapered at the roots.

Growing site   A sunny, open position.

Soil   Deep, fertile and sandy for long specimens. The short-rooted varieties will grow well in slightly heavier soil. Do not add heavy manure to the soil; carrots grown in heavy soil or where organic matter is not well rotted will become misshapen. If your soil is unsuitable, carrots also do well in grow bags or containers, but choose short-rooted varieties.

Sowing   If sowing under cover (greenhouse or cloche), sow in late winter or early spring; if sowing outdoors, wait until late spring when frosts have passed and the soil has had time to warm up.

Make a drill 1 cm (½ in) deep and sow seeds very thinly. To prevent sowing too thickly, try mixing seed with sand before sprinkling along the drill. Cover with a fine layer of soil, firm down gently and water in. Space drills 15 cm (6 in) apart.

Germination   17 days.

Spacing   Space plants 5–7.5 cm (2–3 in) apart. It's best to plant them closer rather than further apart, as this will prevent the need to hoe.

Thinning   Thin out seedlings when they are large enough to handle.

Sowing to harvesting   Early crop: 12 weeks; maincrop: 16 weeks.

Pests and diseases   *Carrot fly*: the worst enemy of carrots. The larvae burrow into the surface of the root and you can't see any signs of damage from the top; it's only when you pull the carrots up that you realize what damage they've done. The carrot fly is invisible and flies just above the ground. When it detects the scent of the carrot, it flies in and lays its eggs. You can buy a fine mesh specifically for deterring carrot fly, but net curtains work just as well. Try planting onions, chives and marigolds alongside your carrots, which are believed to help deter carrot fly.

Weeding   Weed carefully and try not to disturb the foliage.

Watering   Water if the soil is particularly dry, but take care not to overwater. Keep the soil moisture consistent, as a sudden watering or downpour on dry soil can cause the carrots to split.

Harvesting   When the foliage has begun to wilt, gently remove the soil around the base of the leaves and check for size. Ease out the carrots with a fork, or pull gently upwards if the soil is dry. Lift carrots in early winter if you intend storing them.

Storing   Remove excess soil and throw away or eat the damaged carrots immediately. Cut the leaves approximately 1 cm (½ in) above the tops and place the carrots between layers of sand in a sturdy box; don't let them touch each other. They should keep until the following spring.

Carrots freeze well. Blanch for 5 minutes before draining, cooling and sealing in plastic bags, then freeze. They will keep fresh in the refrigerator for up to two weeks.

OPPOSITE: *Carrots are sweeter when eaten soon after picking.*

Beetroot

This crop is very easy to grow, it's low maintenance and produces beautiful blood-red roots topped with edible green leaves with deep-red veins running through them that can be used as salad leaves.

Beetroot can be susceptible to bolting, in which case you'll see a stem creeping out between the leaves, signalling that the plant will no longer be any good, so simply dig it up and throw it away. If possible, buy a bolt-hardy variety, specified on the seed packet.

There is no need to thin if the seeds have been planted at the correct spacing in the ground. Each seed produces three or four roots, which don't develop at the same rate. There is usually a dominant one that can be picked first, allowing the others to grow on.

Dispense with any preconceived ideas that beetroot is only good for pickling – it's such a versatile ingredient. Baby beets are delicious eaten raw. Try grating them into salads or roast the larger ones with a splash of olive oil and chopped garlic.

Tips Don't let your beetroot grow too large, as they'll lose some of their flavour.

• If you're pickling the beetroot and want the root to stay whole, make sure you pick it before it gets too large to fit into your jars.

Best varieties Bolthardy.

Growing site Open, sunny position.

Soil Beetroot likes a neutral soil with neither too much lime nor too much acid. It needs to be fairly soft, without too much clay or sand. Mulch the site before planting.

Sowing Sow early spring to late summer.

The seeds have a corky texture and can be slow to germinate. Ideally, soak seeds overnight to germinate, but it's not essential.

Beetroot can be sown up to four weeks before the last frosts, and can be planted under glass from late winter. Sow short rows every 14 days for a continuous crop.

BELOW: The whole of a beetroot plant can be eaten; the deep red-veined leaves make a delicious warm salad.

Germination Approximately 2 weeks at a minimum of 7°C (45°F).

Spacing Sow seeds 2 cm (¾ in) deep, 5–10 cm (2–4 in) apart.

Thinning If you have planted in seed trays, thin as soon as the first true leaves appear. If left too late, roots can distort or not develop adequately for a good crop. There is no need to thin out if you have planted the seeds in the ground.

Sowing to harvesting 8–16 weeks.

Pests and diseases Beetroot has no common diseases, but it can develop fungal leaf spot.

Weeding Weed by hand or hoe carefully between the rows. Try not to scuff the plant with the hoe or trowel, as the roots can bleed.

Watering Water every day until the leaves start to sprout. If there is no rain, continue to water every few days. Once the plants' leaves have established, the root system will gather its own moisture from the soil.

In dry spells, water established plants every 10–14 days. Don't overwater or the plant will produce fine leaves but a poor root. Lack of water will produce woody roots.

Harvesting You will be able to see some of the root and you'll get an idea of its size. Harvest when the roots have reached the size of a satsuma/clementine. They can be left in the ground to grow until autumn, but if left to grow too long they will develop a woody texture.

Dig up baby beetroot when they're around the size of a golf ball. Lift the roots gently with a fork before you pull them up to loosen the soil; take care not to damage the roots if you're planning on storing.

Storing Beetroots will store throughout the winter. They must be dry and clean when stored. Wait until the soil is dry before harvesting for storage, dust off the soil and wipe clean with a dry cloth. Twist off the foliage a short distance from the root – you may need to wear rubber gloves, as the deep red juice can stain your hands and clothes. Place the beetroot in layers, not touching each other, in moist, sand-filled boxes in a cool, dry shed.

BELOW: *Take care when digging up, as the plant can bleed and stain your hands or clothes.*

Parsnips

A popular root vegetable, parsnips are hardy and easy to grow. When roasted, they develop a sweet, caramelized flavour, and are delicious cooked in olive oil and then sprinkled with grated Parmesan cheese.

They need little attention when growing and the short-rooted varieties can be grown on patios in deep pots. They are hardy and a little frost will even improve their flavour.

Tips Parsnips are related to carrots and are slow to germinate. They're unlikely to germinate in the cold, so choose a warm spot when sowing from seed.

• If you leave a few unharvested roots in the ground, their spring flowers will attract predatory insects such as hoverflies.

Best varieties *Gladiator AGM*: an early variety and easy to grow; *Hollow Crown Improved*: a long variety often used for exhibition.

Growing site Either sun or light shade.

Soil Deep, sandy, fertile and stone-free soil is best, although there are short, stubby varieties that will grow in stony soil. Parsnips prefer soil that has been dug with well-rotted manure and has a fine texture; avoid using fresh manure.

Sowing Sow seeds from late winter to mid-spring directly into the ground.

Germination 10–28 days.

Thinning When seedlings are large enough to handle, pinch out to leave the strongest plants if they're looking too crowded.

Spacing Sow seeds in 2-cm (¾-in) deep drills, 20–25 cm (8–10 in) apart. Sow a pinch of three or four seeds at 13–15-cm (5–6-in) intervals. Water generously with a fine spray.

Sowing to harvesting 34 weeks.

Pests and diseases The plants may occasionally be bothered by celery fly, which can be squashed between the fingers if found.

Weeding Hoe regularly to keep down weeds. Take care not to touch the crowns of the growing plants.

Watering Requires a moist soil, so water during dry spells. Water little and often to keep moisture levels even.

Harvesting Harvest when the leaves start to die down in the autumn to early spring or check the size by gently digging around the base of the plant. Dig up as required. Gently loosen the soil and pull the root up gently, taking care not to spike it with your fork. A potato fork is excellent for lifting parsnips, as it has flatter prongs that don't damage the crop.

Storing Throw away or eat the damaged roots immediately. If storing parsnips for long-term use, remove the excess soil and cut the leaves approximately 1 cm (½ in) above the tops. Place the parsnips between layers of sand in a sturdy box; don't let them touch each other. They will keep until the following spring. For short-term use, store in a plastic bag in the refrigerator for up to two weeks.

LEFT: Parsnips are hardy and easy to grow.

Radishes

Famously easy to grow, these pretty red, pink or white crunchy balls or tubes are welcome additions to summer salads. Radishes are a great crop for filling spaces between rows of carrots and peas, or intercropping with slow-growing plants such as carrots, parsnips or onions.

Tips Rapid growth is vital for a good yield. Water well in summer months to give the plants the best chance of producing a juicy crop, otherwise they can become tough and woody.

• Use a 'mixed radish' seed that matures at different times.

• Don't sow too many at a time because they're very quick to grow and will easily go to seed if they're not eaten.

Best varieties *Scarlet Globe*: a quick-maturing variety; *French Breakfast 3 AGM*: a popular variety, long and mild if harvested early, peppery and woody if harvested late.

Growing site Prefers a sunny spot for spring sowing, but needs some shade for summer sowing. Grows well between other vegetables that can offer a little shade.

Soil Radishes thrive in most soils, but prefer it well drained and stone free.

Sowing Summer varieties: sow outdoors in early spring or under cloches in late winter; winter varieties: sow in late summer for harvesting in late autumn onwards. Rake to create a fine surface and remove any stones. Sow seed thinly in drills.

Germination 4–7 days.

Thinning Pinch out to leave stronger seedlings.

Spacing If seedlings look overcrowded, space small varieties at 2.5-cm (1-in) intervals or large varieties at 5–10-cm (2–4-in) intervals.

Sowing to harvesting Summer varieties: 3–6 weeks; winter varieties: 10–12 weeks.

Pests and diseases *Birds*: can be a nuisance to young seedlings; protect the crop with netting if this is a problem.

   Flea beetle: creates small holes in the leaves. Cover with fleece or fine mesh that is beetle-proof.

Weeding Hoe regularly in order to keep weeds under control.

Watering Water if the soil becomes dry.

Harvesting Harvest the tubular varieties when they are around the same size as your thumb. Dig up globe varieties when they are approximately 2.5 cm (1 in) in diameter.

   Leave winter varieties in the ground and use as required, but protect the surface of the soil with some straw or other protection.

Storing For the best flavour, eat immediately. They will keep in a plastic bag in the refrigerator for up to a week, but be sure to dry them first.

RIGHT: *Radishes come in beautiful pinks, reds and whites.*

BRASSICAS

The brassica group includes cabbages, Brussels sprouts, broccoli and cauliflower. They are highly nutritious and have huge health benefits. These beautiful and interesting-looking vegetables have been around for thousands of years. Most brassicas are relatively easy to grow for the beginner gardener with the exception of cauliflower, which needs a little more experience. Brassicas are a particular delicacy for birds and insects, so try using a bird deterrent or covering the crops with mesh.

Brussels sprouts

This brassica has suffered a bad press. Previous generations have often boiled them so that all their taste disappears to leave just a soggy mess that no longer resembles anything like the vegetable growing on the plant.

Tips Brussels sprouts won't grow well in loose soil – the ground must be firm and the soil rich in humus.

• Frosts make Brussels sprouts taste sweeter, so don't pick the crop until after the first frost (that's if you can bear to leave them on the plant that long).

• Cabbage root fly can be a pest. Avoid forking up the soil before planting and firm down well after transplanting seedlings. Keep an eye on the soil, and if it becomes loose during growth, gently firm down around the base of the stem using your heel.

• Earth up around the stems in autumn to give extra protection from high winds in winter.

The Brussels sprout is a mini gem. Picked straight from the garden and cooked well, sprouts are morsels of delicacy and deserve appreciation as a delightful winter vegetable. And once the sprouts have been harvested, you can also cook the top of the plant as you would cabbage.

Best varieties *Revenge AGM*: high yielding and firm; *Red Delicious*: an interesting red variety, ready to harvest from late autumn; *Peer Gynt*: a high-yielding and popular variety.
Growing site Sunny position, sheltered from winds.
Soil Ideally, Brussels sprouts prefer a firm soil with a pH of 6–7.5, but they grow well in most soils. Prepare the soil in autumn by digging in lots of well-rotted manure.
Sowing Sow early to mid-spring.

Sow in cell trays or prepare a seedbed by raking over the surface to produce a fine, crumbly texture. Make a 1-cm (½-in) deep drill, sprinkle the seed thinly and cover with soil. Gently firm the soil by patting down with your heel. Transplant seedlings when they are approximately 10–15 cm (4–6 in) high. Support plants with a stake approximately 5 x 2.5 cm (2 x 1 in).

Germination 7–12 days.

Spacing Leave 76 cm (30 in) between the plants and the rows to aid air circulation, make picking easier and help prevent fungal diseases. If you have a small plot, space them 45 cm (18 in) apart.

Sowing to harvesting Early varieties: 28 weeks; late varieties: 36 weeks.

Pests and diseases *Cabbage whitefly*: protect with fine netting or fleece.

　　Cabbage root fly; aphids.

Weeding Hoe regularly around the plants and between rows to prevent weeds developing. Brussels sprouts can stay in the ground for some time, so shouldn't have to compete with weeds for nutrients in the soil.

Watering Water well as the plant is developing and during dry spells.

Harvesting Even though the early varieties are ready from early autumn, leave them in the ground until after the first frosts to maximize their flavour.

　　Harvest when the sprouts are firm and the size of a walnut. Start removing from the bottom of the plant and work your way up using a sharp knife.

　　If you pick on demand, you should be able to harvest from one plant from early autumn to early the following spring.

Storing Best picked and eaten fresh, as they don't store particularly well. They can be frozen, but reduce the cooking time after freezing or they may turn soft and mushy.

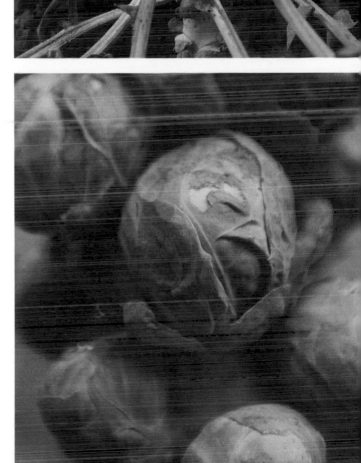

ABOVE RIGHT: Dark green little nodules of delight.

RIGHT: Brussels sprouts are an underrated brassica – pick fresh, straight from the plant, then cook and eat them while they still have a slight crunch.

Cauliflower

Once a staple item of the Sunday roast plate, cauliflower is famous for the dish cauliflower cheese. However, in the UK, cauliflower production has declined by nearly a third during the last decade and been superseded by imported and arguably more exciting vegetables.

Many people have simply forgotten how good cauliflowers are and there is a wealth of new, inspiring recipes now available, offering us the encouragement to start eating this beautiful vegetable again.

Cauliflowers are not only white; you can get yellow and even purple varieties.

Tips As the plant begins to grow, support the stems with wooden stakes approximately 5 x 2.5 cm (2 x 1 in).

• Plant seeds in cell trays if possible and transplant seedlings outdoors when large enough in order to protect them from slugs and snails, which are rather fond of the juicy, young plants.

• With summer varieties, curve a few leaves over the developing head to protect it from the sun. In the winter, protect from frosts by breaking off a few leaves and draping over the developing heads.

Best varieties *All The Year Round; Autumn Giant; Pavilion; Violet Queen.*

Growing site Choose a sunny site with firm soil. Avoid planting in a frost pocket or low-lying ground. Also avoid planting near overhanging trees or tall hedges, or the plants will be poor. Winter varieties prefer a sunny but sheltered rather than exposed site and protection from north and east winds. Summer crops prefer a site in full sun and sheltered from winds.

Soil If possible, prepare in the autumn and dig in plenty of well-rotted organic matter or garden compost. Cauliflowers need a rich, dark and firm soil. Rake the soil flat and then press gently with your heel along the seedbed. Loose soil will cause bad root development, so while the plant is growing, check that the soil isn't becoming loose and firm down gently around the plant with your heel if necessary.

Sowing Sow midsummer for harvesting the following spring; mid-spring for summer and autumn harvesting.

Check the date for sowing on the seed packet and don't be tempted to sow earlier than the specified date or the plants may bolt. Sow in cell trays, two or three seeds per section, and cover with sifted soil. Water in with a fine spray.

Germination 7–12 days.

Thinning Thin when seedlings have five or six leaves. Rake the ground so that the soil is even and flat, then firm the soil by pressing down gently with your heel. Water in after planting.

Mulch the soil around plants with well-rotted manure or garden compost three weeks after planting, drenching with water afterwards.

Spacing Leave 30 cm (12 in) between plants to allow air circulation and help prevent diseases.

Sowing to harvesting Summer and autumn varieties: 18–24 weeks; winter varieties: 40–50 weeks.

Pests and diseases *Cabbage root fly:* growing garlic or chives near cauliflowers is reputed to discourage this pest.

Cabbage whitefly: cover with fine netting when the plants are young to protect them against this pest, as well as pigeons (see below).

Pigeons: protect as for cabbage whitefly (see above).

Slugs and snails; caterpillars; club root.

Weeding Weed regularly and gently by hand or hoe. Take care not to disturb the soil, as the plants prefer firm soil.

Watering Cauliflowers must never dry out, particularly when plants are young, causing small heads to form.

Harvesting To avoid a cauliflower glut, begin harvesting while still small. Cut before the florets have started to separate.

Harvest in the morning while the plants still have dew on them, but wait until the middle of the day in winter.

Storing Store for up to three weeks by lifting the plants with their roots, shaking off the soil and hanging upside down in a cool shed. Spray occasionally with a fine mist spray.

Cauliflowers will keep in a plastic bag in the refrigerator for up to two weeks.

BELOW: Cauliflower heads hide behind a blanket of curved leaves that protect them while they're growing.

Kale

A traditional cold-climate vegetable, kale has been grown for centuries. In fact, in 19th-century Scotland, 'kail' was a generic term used for 'dinner'. It's both tasty and nutritious, being a good source of vitamins A, C and E. The leaves should be picked when they're young and tender, as the larger, older leaves tend to taste bitter.

Kale is such an attractive-looking vegetable that it's often planted along with ornamental plants in the garden. If you trim off the young, tender leaves, it will make the plant more bushy and this cut-and-come-again approach means that you'll have a thriving crop throughout the year.

Tips Remove any yellowing leaves from the base of the plant, providing plenty of air circulation that helps avoid unwelcome pests and diseases.

- If the plants are looking droopy and unattractive in winter, don't worry as when spring appears they will quickly produce new fresh shoots.

- Kale prefers cool temperatures and will be sweetened by a touch of frost.

Best varieties *Thousand-Headed, Red Bor, Cavolo Nero, Red Russian.*

Growing site Kale is more adaptable than most other brassicas and doesn't mind a little shade. It's completely frost hardy and the flavour even improves with a little frost.

Soil Kale grows well in any soil, but if you dig in a little well-rotted manure or compost it will help.

Sowing Sow curly-leaved kale in mid-spring for cropping the following winter; leaf and spear or plain-leaved kale in late spring; rape kale in the early summer.

LEFT: Kale is not just for the vegetable bed; the curly, flirty leaves also give your flower bed a sense of fun and flavour.

There's no need to dig the ground; simply rake the soil before sowing to create a fine, crumbly texture. Make a 1-cm (½-in) drill and scatter in the seeds. Use a bed that has been used for peas, early potatoes or summer crops.

Rape kale is not keen on being transplanted, so sow directly into its permanent growing space in early summer for a crop the following spring.

Germination 7–12 days.

Thinning Plant seedlings when they are six to eight weeks old or around 10–15 cm (4–6 in) high. Water the plants before transplanting to their final growing positions, then water the seedlings well after planting.

Spacing Thin seedlings at 7.5 cm (3 in) apart in rows 45 cm (18 in) apart.

Because rape kale is planted directly into its permanent growing space, sow seeds at 45-cm (18-in) intervals along the rows and place rows 45 cm (18 in) apart.

Sowing to harvesting 30–35 weeks.

Pests and diseases Kale is very resistant to most diseases and pests, but *aphids*, *whitefly* and *cabbage caterpillar* can cause problems.

Weeding Hoe around the stems carefully and remove any dead leaves from the lower stems.

Watering Water well in hot, dry spells and in cooler spells water approximately every 10 days.

Harvesting Pick young leaves from autumn through to mid-spring, a few at a time, using a sharp knife. Picking from the crown of the plant from late autumn onwards will encourage the side shoots, which can then be picked from spring onwards. Kale tastes best when harvested young and tender. Discard old leaves, as they can taste bitter and tough.

Rape kale is an earlier crop and can be picked from early to late spring.

Storing Pick and eat immediately for the best flavour. Kale will keep in the refrigerator for a few days, but it tends to become increasingly bitter and strong flavoured the longer it's stored. Leave on the plant if possible until you're ready to eat it.

Cabbages

Cabbage hasn't enjoyed the best of reputations over the years. Boiled half to death in school canteens and with the lingering smell of boiled cabbage in our parents' kitchens, it's not surprising that some of us have been put off it. Think again – there are now a host of interesting varieties for you to grow and use in stir-fries and coleslaw or as a hot winter salad, or to stuff or bake.

Cabbages are also incredibly good for your health, being high in vitamin C and full of antioxidants. While they're best eaten when freshly picked, they also store very well in straw-lined boxes.

Able to be harvested all year round, cabbages thrive in cold, damp climates and are especially valuable for growing during the time of year when fresh vegetables from the garden are scarce. They take up a lot of space in the garden, which many people find discouraging, but they are very hardy and come in a range of colours and textures. Do give them a try.

Best varieties *Protovoy* (Savoy); *January King* (red-tinged leaves); *Advantage F1* (spring); *Red Drumhead* (red).

Growing site Choose a sunny site. Cabbages will grow in most temperate climates.

Tips Don't sow too many at once; grow just a small row a few weeks at a time.

• Firm down any plants where soil becomes loosened in winter from frosts or wind.

• Place a collar around the stems of cabbages to protect them from cabbage root fly.

• To protect from frosts and wind, earth up the soil around the base of each plant.

• Remove any dead leaves as they appear.

Soil Most soils are suitable for growing cabbages, but as with all brassicas, club root is a potential problem, and the pH of the soil is an important factor in guarding against it. The ideal range is 6–7.5 pH, so if possible check the soil pH (see page 21) and add lime if necessary to bring the pH level up.

Cabbages prefer a medium to light soil that will retain a reasonable amount of water but that drains well.

Rake the soil to make an even surface. Cabbages need a firm soil to grow well, so firm before planting and press the soil down gently once the plants are in the ground.

Sowing Cabbages are grouped by season and sowing times vary accordingly; check the seed packet for recommended sowing times.

Summer cabbages: sow from late winter to early spring; autumn cabbages: from early to late spring; winter cabbages: when summer arrives; spring cabbages: mid- to late summer.

Sow outside very thinly in drills 1 cm (½ in) deep. If starting off in a seed tray, sprinkle seeds across the tray, allowing a finger width between seeds. Cover the seeds with a thin layer of fine compost, water in and leave in a sunny place, making sure the compost remains moist.

Germination 7–12 days.

Spacing Sow in rows 15 cm (6 in) apart.

Thinning When seedlings are large enough to handle and have five or six leaves, plant in rows approximately 7.5 cm (3 in) apart. Water the roots thoroughly and firm the soil around the plants.

If the variety has large heads, leave approximately 30–45 cm (12–18 in) between plants. For spring cabbages, thin plants to approximately 10-cm (4-in) intervals in rows 30 cm (12 in) apart.

Sowing to harvesting Spring varieties: 35 weeks; summer/winter varieties: 10 weeks.

Pests and diseases Birds: a problem when plants are young; cover the cabbage bed with fleece or fine netting to protect against them, as well as butterflies (see opposite).

Cabbage caterpillar: the cabbage white butterfly lays eggs on the leaves and the caterpillars eat the leaves; protect as for birds opposite.

Cabbage root fly; club root.

Weeding Cabbages stay in the ground for some time, so it's essential to keep watch for emerging weeds and hoe regularly around the plants. Putting a layer of garden compost around, but not touching, the plants will conserve moisture and prevent weeds taking over.

Watering Cabbages can produce split heads if they have inconsistent moisture. They are very hardy and if watered well as seedlings will last some time without watering; approximately every 10 days as a guide. Give extra water when the weather is hot and dry and a liquid feed when the heads begin to emerge.

Harvesting When the hearts of your cabbages are firm, cut as required with a sharp knife. Cut a cross into the cut stumps of spring and summer cabbages to produce a bonus second crop of smaller cabbages.

Storing Cabbages can be harvested in autumn and stored for winter use. Cut off the roots and the stem and remove the outer leaves. Stored in a straw-lined box in a cool, dry place, they should keep until early spring.

BELOW: A satisfying brassica to grow and most welcome when other crops are sparse.

Broccoli

Broccoli is indeed a superfood. Studies have shown that men who ate broccoli more than once a week were 45 per cent less likely to develop stage III and IV prostate cancers. Drusius, son of Roman Emperor Tiberius, gorged exclusively on broccoli for an entire month and as a result his urine turned bright green, whereupon his father admonished him for, as he put it, living precariously. Drusius finally managed to kick the habit.

It's a hardy vegetable that's great for growing in cold climates, as it stands up well to hail, rain and snow. The heads of tightly bound immature flowers are eaten before they start to open out into flowers. There are three types: calabrese, which is harvested in the autumn, and purple and white, for harvesting the following spring. Calabrese types are green and have round heads; the purple and white types have a taller, more tree-like appearance with their stem resembling a trunk topped with a head of leaves.

The garden variety of choice is often purple sprouting broccoli, since this is the hardiest. Purple and white varieties are best planted out in the summer months ready for the following spring. All types of broccoli are high yielding and perfect for filling in the gaps between Brussels sprouts or spring cabbages.

Tips Broccoli will sometimes work the soil loose, so the ground needs to be firm, as loose soil will develop poor root growth.

• Broccoli and other brassicas such as cauliflower and cabbage grow best in the previous year's potato bed.

Best varieties Calabrese – *Express Corona*: a fast-yielding plant that produces a head around 45 days after planting; purple sprouting – *Red Arrow*: high yielding with good flavour; white sprouting – *Early* or *Late*.

Because of the big differences in sowing to harvesting times for different types of broccoli, it's important to check the instructions on the seed packet so that you choose the appropriate variety for your needs.

Growing site Broccoli prefers full sun, but will tolerate partial shade well. As broccoli usually stays in the ground over the winter, avoid low-lying positions where the soil may become waterlogged.

Soil Broccoli prefers a rich soil. Dig in well-rotted manure or good-quality organic matter in the autumn. As the soil needs to be alkaline to avoid club root, it's a good idea to carry out a pH test (see page 21).

Sowing Sow early varieties in mid-spring; late varieties in midsummer.

Calabrese doesn't transplant very well, so try to sow in situ. Prepare a seedbed by raking over the surface to produce a fine, crumbly texture. Make a 1-cm (½-in) deep drill. Sprinkle the seed thinly and cover with soil. Gently firm the soil by patting down with your heel.

Germination 7–10 days.

Spacing Thin at 7.5 cm (3 in) apart. Leave 30 cm (12 in) between calabrese plants and 45 cm (18 in) between purple and white sprouting types. The wide spacing allows plenty of air circulation and helps prevent diseases.

Thinning Water the seedbed of purple and white varieties before transplanting. Thin when the seedlings have reached around 10–15 cm (4–6 in) high. Rake so that the soil is even, then firm by pressing down gently with your heel. Water in after transplanting.

Sowing to harvesting Calabrese: 12 weeks; purple and white sprouting: 44 weeks.

Pests and diseases *Slugs and snails*: can be a problem in the early stages.

Pigeons and other birds: these will also make a meal of young seedlings; try covering them with a fine mesh while the leaves are still young and tender.

Caterpillars: a common problem, so make regular checks to see if the leaves are developing any telltale holes.

Whitefly: this can develop underneath the leaves of broccoli. Either spray with soft soap or use derris powder.

Club root: this is a common problem with all types of brassicas.

Weeding Weed regularly by hand or gently with a hoe as soon as weeds appear.

Watering Water your broccoli crop throughout dry weather and apply a mulch to keep the soil moist. Watering is especially important when the heads are forming.

Harvesting Harvest before the flower buds have opened or they will taste woody. Cut the central spear, which will appear as a head. Broccoli should be cut off around halfway down the stem. Harvest regularly for around a six-week period to ensure a continuing crop.

Storing It will keep in a plastic bag in the refrigerator for up to three days. Broccoli freezes well; blanch, drain and cool beforehand.

BELOW: *This remarkable vegetable is packed full of vitamins, is easy to grow, delicious and a staple of many roast dinners.*

LEGUMES

The legume family includes peas, broad beans and French and runner beans. They are mainly vegetables that have a pod and their fruits or pulses within are eaten either fresh or dried for storage. Lentils, beans and soya also fall within this group. They are all easy to grow but some will need a very simple structure of twigs or canes for support.

Peas

There is something very satisfying about opening the plump pods of peas, popping them open to reveal the little round seed balls. Children are particularly fond of podding peas – an excellent way to enlighten them on the art of growing vegetables and using them in the kitchen.

Peas were the first vegetable ever to be canned, but they are now mostly bought frozen. As soon as peas are picked from the plant, their sugar content starts to turn to starch and they begin to lose their tenderness, so they're best eaten when fresh and cooked quickly to retain their deliciously sweet flavour. Mangetout and sugar snap varieties can be eaten whole, pod and all.

> *Tips* Peas are climbers and can reach a height of 2 m (6½ ft). Support them by using a variety of twigs and small branches in your beds or pots, putting the supports in position as soon as the seedlings are around 7.5 cm (3 in) high.
>
> • When the plant has finished cropping, don't dig it up; instead, cut the stem to ground level, as the small white nodules at the roots are full of nitrogen-fixing bacteria and if left in the ground will rot and provide valuable nitrogen for the next crop.

They are easy to grow and are best sown with a week or two between each sowing to avoid a glut, although if the weather suddenly turns hot, they'll all be ready to harvest at once and you'll have to find a variety of recipes to use them straight away or freeze them immediately after picking. They also grow very well in containers, particularly dwarf varieties.

Pea varieties are grouped according to the time they take to mature: first earlies take around 12 weeks to mature, second earlies 13–14 weeks and maincrops 15–16 weeks.

Best varieties Early – *Early Onward*: high-yielding and popular variety; maincrop – *Lord Chancellor*: high yielding with dark green, pointed pods; sugar snap – *Sugar Lord*: tall and vigorous with a high yield; mangetout – *Oregon Sugarpod*: produces flat pods to be eaten whole.

Growing site Prefers a sunny position.

Soil Early crops like a warm, dry soil. Maincrops prefer a rich, moisture-retentive soil to which well-rotted manure has been added.

Sowing Sow early spring to midsummer, depending on the variety.

Sow directly into the soil in weekly or fortnightly successions in 5-cm (2-in) drills, in rows 38–120 cm (15–48 in) apart. Plenty of space between the rows will aid air circulation and make weeding easier. Immediately after sowing you will need to protect the seeds from birds and mice.

Find some twiggy branches and place them over the soil surface or buy some netting, fleece or chicken wire.

Spacing Sow at 13–15-cm (5–6-in) intervals along the row.

Germination 7–10 days.

Sowing to harvesting Autumn sowing: 32 weeks; spring sowing: 12–16 weeks.

Pests and diseases *Birds and mice*: both will devour young shoots if not protected.

Slugs: these will attack the young shoots, so the use of supports is vital in getting the shoots off the ground and as high and out of the way as soon as possible.

Powdery mildew: a common problem in late summer; resistant varieties are available.

Pea thrip: leaves a silvery coating on the pod. Pick the affected pods and destroy them.

Weeding Regularly weed by hoe or hand, taking care not to damage the plants.

Watering Peas are very thirsty plants and like plenty of moisture. Keep the soil well watered, particularly during dry spells, and mulch around the base of the plants with well-rotted manure.

Harvesting When pods feel plump, harvest with a sharp knife or scissors every two or three days, which will encourage new pods to develop. Begin at the bottom of the stem and work upwards. Even if the peas have gone past their best, still pick them to allow room for new pods to grow.

Pick mangetout and sugar snap varieties when they reach around 7.5 cm (3 in) long.

Storing Peas are definitely best eaten immediately, but if you have a glut and need to store them, try freezing them. They'll keep in the refrigerator for up to a week in a sealed plastic bag.

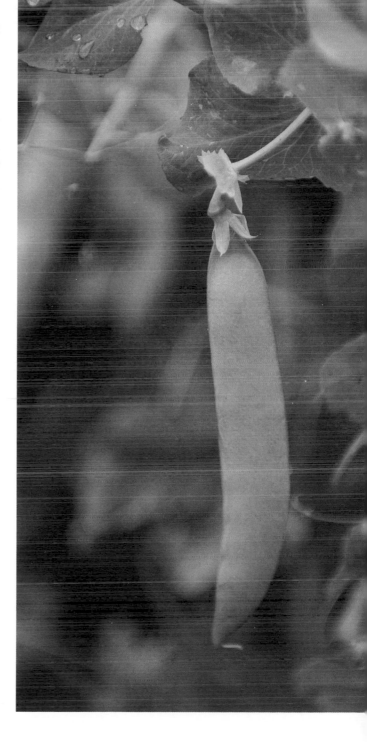

RIGHT: *Pick and eat peas straight away for the sweetest flavour.*

Broad beans

This is the perfect vegetable for the novice grower, needing only a little help to grow into highly attractive and productive plants. They produce pretty clusters of small white flowers and attract a variety of pollinators. As the flowers fade, fat, shiny pods begin to develop. The beans are the seed of the plant and can be eaten raw or cooked.

One of the first crops to plant, they can be sown in the autumn and be ready to pick in late spring.

When the plant is around 15 cm (6 in) tall, place some canes or supports along the bed and attach string between the uprights (see page 86). As the beans get taller, they can be tied to the string for support.

Tips When the first pods begin to appear at the base of the plant, pinch out the growing tips. This concentrates the plant's energy on pod formation. Twist off the top of the stem and two leaves.

• After the plant has finished cropping, dig it into the soil to provide valuable green manure.

Best varieties Many of the broad bean varieties have been around for over 100 years, which generally means they are stable, reliable and pest resistant. Try *Bunyard's Exhibition*.

Common varieties are *The Sutton*, a dwarf variety that doesn't usually require supports and can be used for autumn sowing, but does best if protected with a cloche and planted early. Also recommended are *Masterpiece Green Longpod* and *Aquadulce Claudia*; the latter is good for autumn or early spring sowing.

Growing site Fairly sunny, sheltered from the wind and somewhere that wasn't planted with beans the previous year. Former potato plots make the best growing sites. Try to plant when conditions are fine if possible, as the plants don't like persistently wet or cold weather, but they can be planted in relatively cold conditions, down to 2°C (36°F).

Soil Preferably rich and heavy, but broad beans grow well in most soils provided that it's not waterlogged. Enrich the soil before planting with compost or well-rotted manure.

Sowing If sowing inside, plant one seed per pot. In drills outside, plant 20 cm (8 in) apart. Broad beans can be planted in the ground in the autumn if you choose a hardy variety and want an early crop in the spring, but only do this if you have a sheltered spot or you'll get heavy losses. Alternatively, sow in early spring inside or outside, depending on the weather, for a summer crop. When transferring from the greenhouse to outside, acclimatize seedlings before planting out.

Germination 7–14 days.

Spacing Plant 5 cm (2 in) deep in drills approximately 20 cm (8 in) apart. If planting in more than one row, allow 20 cm (8 in) between each row.

Sowing to harvesting Approximately 14 weeks.

Pests and diseases *Black fly*: likes the young shoots of broad beans.

Aphids: if you spot these, pinch out the tips of the plants. Try planting marigolds as a companion plant, reputed to lure the aphids away from the broad bean and onto the marigold flower. Nasturtiums planted near the beans will attract aphids away from the beans. Ladybirds are beneficial because they eat aphids, so try to encourage them if you can.

Vine weavil: a common problem; serrated edges to young leaves may be evidence of weavils munching around them.

Weeding Hoe regularly to keep down weeds, particularly when the plant is young.

Watering Unnecessary until the flowers appear. If there is a dry spell and the pods have appeared, give the plants a good watering.

Harvesting Best picked when you can feel the

beans in the fleshy pods. Don't leave them to grow to their maximum size or they can be tough to eat. Begin by picking them when the pods are 5–7.5 cm (2–3 in) long and cook them whole. Pick pods for shelling when the beans are showing through the pod but before the scar on the bean has become discoloured or black; it should be white or green. Pick using a downward motion and a twist. Try to harvest the beans when it's dry. If you let the beans carry on growing until the plant dies off, you can pick the seeds and use them for next year's sowing.

Storing Broad beans freeze well. Blanch for 3 minutes, then drain and cool before freezing. Fresh beans should keep for up to a week in a plastic bag in the refrigerator.

BELOW: Broad beans look very decorative in the vegetable garden; they have little white flowers that attract bees and other welcome insects.

making a broad bean support

Broad beans can grow over 1 m (3¼ ft) high and the stems will need supporting, as when the flowers develop into beans the weight of the pods can easily snap the stems. There are different methods of making a support, depending on how many plants you have and if there's one row or two, or more. The twine needs to be fairly tight to straighten the poles; use a length of twine on each side of a row.

1 Push a bamboo or other suitable sturdy pole at each end of the broad bean row and one in the middle.

2 Tie garden twine (or string) at 15-cm (6-in) intervals to one of the poles about 15 cm (6 in) from the base.

3 Take the twine to the centre pole around the outside of the plants so that they are supported inwards.

4 Wrap the twine around the pole to secure, then continue to the third pole, wind it around and take it all the way back to the first pole. Tie in a knot to secure.

5 As the plants grow, support them by tying the stems to the string.

French beans

The lush, green leaves of French beans look fabulous when they're dripping with their fine, tubular pods. Besides green, they also come in yellow, purple and cream. French beans are usually eaten whole, but if you leave the pods to mature, they will produce fresh haricot beans inside. Most of their growing takes place vertically, allowing them to be cultivated in a small space.

For tall varieties, you will need to build a wigwam of canes or provide support for the beans as they grow. Shorter varieties can be supported with twigs or pea sticks.

French beans grow slowly if the weather is cool and will be at risk from slug attacks. It's far better if you can bring them on inside in late spring or early summer, when they stand a better chance of growing quick and tall, thus avoiding the slugs once they are transplanted outside.

Sowing Early crop: sow mid- to late spring; maincrop: late spring to early summer.

Start the seeds off inside if possible. Sow two seeds per pot 5 cm (2 in) deep. Transplant once the seedlings are 7.5 cm (3 in) tall.

Germination 7–14 days.

Spacing Plant 10 cm (4 in) apart with 45 cm (18 in) between each row.

Sowing to harvesting 8–12 weeks.

Weeding Hoe to keep weeds down, particularly during early growth where slugs can be hiding under nearby weeds.

Pests and diseases Slugs, snails and birds will all attack young plants.

Watering Keeping the roots of the plant moist is essential for plant development. Water well and at regular intervals.

Harvesting When the pods are approximately 10 cm (4 in) long and firm, snap them cleanly off the plant. Hold the stems as you snap the pods or you could damage the plants, or use a pair of scissors. Pick often to prevent the pods from maturing and to encourage new pods to form.

Storing Keep in a plastic bag in the refrigerator for up to a week. They freeze very well; blanch for 2–3 minutes before draining, cooling and freezing.

Tips Protect early crops with fleece or a cloche if growing directly outside, as the plant is not frost hardy and prefers warm soil.

• To avoid birds from stripping the young seedlings, surround the young plants with bushy twigs.

• Mulch plants around the stem to give them some stability.

• Build a means of support for the plants (see opposite), growing one plant per cane or pole. Climbing varieties can also be grown up trellises or over arches.

Best varieties Barlotta Lingua di Fuoco; Delinea; Kenyan Bean AGM.

Growing site Choose a sunny, sheltered spot. The plants have tender foliage and can grow tall, so they need protection from winds.

Soil Light, rich soil.

BELOW: When cooking purple French beans, try adding a little vinegar to the water to help retain the colour.

Runner beans

Runner beans are highly popular and a typical feature of kitchen gardens. As well as producing an abundant crop, they look wonderfully attractive for a long period of time during the summer with their pretty flowers and long, dripping pods. The tall varieties are prolific and need supports for their lush growth, while the dwarf varieties tend to crop earlier in the year.

Runner beans are delicious when picked and cooked immediately in lightly salted boiling water, served with just a knob of butter. More mature beans tend to have tough 'strings' running down their sides, which need to be trimmed before cooking, but if the beans are young, the whole bean will be tender and it therefore won't need de-stringing.

Tips It's very tempting to plant a long row of runner beans, but the secret is to grow only a limited number to avoid a glut.

• For a particularly lush-looking crop, grow two plants per supporting cane.

• Pinch out the growing tips when 60 cm (2 ft) high and again at 1.2 m (4 ft) high to encourage growth of productive side shoots.

• Keep dwarf variety pods off the ground by supporting them with twiggy sticks.

• There's an old wives' tale that says: 'See them twice in May'; if you plant runner beans at the beginning of May, you should see them come through by the end of May.

• Sometimes you can have problems getting the pods to set, particularly during a dry period. Try watering the flowers, which produce the beans, in order to trigger bean formation.

Best varieties Desiree, Scarlet Emperor, White Lady, Wisley Magic.

Growing site Sunny and sheltered from winds. Position them in a space where they won't shade other plants.

Soil It's best to improve the soil before planting runner beans. If possible, dig in compost or well-rotted manure a few months before planting. Alternatively, dig a trench in the ground where they are to be planted, add compost or mulch and cover with soil, then sow the seeds or plant the seedlings on top. This will retain the moisture and add nutrients to the soil.

Sowing Start off inside if possible in mid- to late spring. Sow two seeds per pot 5 cm (2 in) deep. Transplant once the seedlings are 7.5 cm (3 in) tall.

If planting directly outside, wait until the risk of frost has passed and the soil has warmed up, then sow 5 cm (2 in) deep, 23 cm (9 in) apart.

Grow beans either on a wigwam of supporting canes or against a trellis.

Germination 7–14 days.

Spacing Allow 46 cm (18 in) between each row.

Sowing to harvesting 12–14 weeks.

Pests and diseases Slugs, snails and birds will all devour young plants.

Weeding Hoe regularly to keep weeds down. Try applying a mulch around the base of the stems to retain moisture and reduce weeds.

Watering Water regularly; the plants need extra moisture particularly once flowers begin to appear.

Harvesting When the beans are approximately 15–20 cm (6–8 in) long and firm, snap off or cut with scissors. They will grow vigorously, so pick them daily to encourage new growth and to prevent them over-maturing.

Storing All beans are best picked and eaten fresh, but they will keep up to a week in a plastic bag in the refrigerator. They also freeze well; blanch for 2–3 minutes before draining, cooling and freezing.

RIGHT: *The tall plants and bright orange flowers of runner beans make a stunning display during summer months.*

ONION FAMILY

Onions are from the allium family. They grow underground with a vertical shoot emerging from the plant above ground. In this popular vegetable family are garlic, shallots, leeks and, of course, onions. They are very easy to grow and fantastic to store for use all year round.

Onions and shallots

The onion is a staple ingredient in almost every cuisine across the globe, and its uses in the kitchen are practically inexhaustible. Onions are easy to grow, can be stored all year round and are rich in vitamin C and beneficial minerals.

A smaller and more aromatic version of the onion, shallots grow in clusters of small bulbs.

Planting sets rather than raising plants from seed is a quicker and more reliable way to cultivate onions and shallots. They grow rapidly – which is a useful asset in cooler climates – and can be successfully planted in the same place each year.

> *Tip* Plant with legumes (peas and beans) to help protect against fungal diseases.

Best varieties Onion – *Red Baron* (red); *Setton*: excellent yield of dark-skinned bulbs; *Sturon*: reliable, excellent flavour and stores well; shallots – *Longor*: long bulbs with good flavour and yield that store well; *Pikant* – strongly flavoured and high yielding.

Growing site An open, sunny site with good drainage.

Soil Onions prefer a slightly sandy soil if possible, but they will thrive in most soils. Their roots will have difficulty penetrating a heavy clay soil. Dig the onion bed in autumn with plenty of well-rotted manure or compost.

Sowing/planting Sow or plant late winter to spring; they are unaffected by frost.

Before planting, rake the surface when the soil is dry to produce a fine, even soil bed. Mark out rows 25–30 cm (10–12 in) apart and push in the sets with a 7.5–10-cm (3–4-in) space between sets. Each set should have the pointed tip uppermost, slightly showing above the soil.

Shallots need to be planted earlier and with wider spacing to allow for the cluster of small bulbs. Space 15 cm (6 in) apart with 25–30 cm (10–12 in) between each row.

Germination 21 days.

Thinning If sowing sets, thinning is unnecessary. If growing from seed, thin to 30 cm (12 in) apart.

Spacing 5–10 cm (2–4 in) apart in rows 30 cm (12 in) apart.

Sowing to harvest Spring sowing: 16–22 weeks; later summer sowing: 40–46 weeks.

Pests and diseases *Birds*: common pests (particularly your hens) when the sets are first planted. You can net them at this stage and remove the nets later when the bulbs have taken hold.

Frost: this can lift the sets; if this becomes a problem, cover with fleece or a cloche. The developing root can also lift the bulb out of the ground; simply push the bulb back in.

Mildew: this can be a problem particularly during a wet spell. Pick off affected leaves.

Onion white rot: indicated by leaves turning yellow and wilting. Destroy the infected plants, as there is no cure, and don't grow onions or garlic on the same site for eight years to allow the disease to die out.

Onion fly: leaves begin to twist and shrivel, and if you open the bulb out, you'll see a collection of maggots at the base. Destroy and burn the plant, and don't put it on the compost.

Weeding Onions and shallots have shallow roots, so weed regularly to avoid competition for nutrients and water and avoid hoeing near the roots, hand weeding instead to avoid root disturbance. Ideally, use an onion hoe, a short-handled tool that gives good control.

Watering Water only if the weather is particularly hot and dry. Mulching is useful and reduces the need for water. Stop watering once the onions have swollen, and if they have already emerged and are sitting on top of the soil, pull back the soil to expose the top of the bulb.

Too much or too little watering can result in the onions bolting.

Harvesting The plant is ready for harvesting when the leaves wilt and turn yellow. Using a garden fork, lift the plant up gently and let the leaves dry out completely.

Storing Either use up onions immediately or allow those intended for storage to dry out. Place them individually on a table or rack, preferably in the sun or in a warm, dry place. Depending on the size of the bulbs, the drying process will take 7–21 days. If some of the foliage is still damp and mushy, try leaving the onions to dry a little longer, or use them straight away. Store either in trays or a pair of tights, or tie them to a length of cord to create an onion string (see overleaf). Stored in a cool, well-lit room, they should keep until the following spring.

Don't store onions that show any sign of disease. Use immediately or destroy the ones severely damaged and beyond use.

BELOW: Onions are ready when the stems start to discolour and droop.

stringing onions

Once they've been allowed to dry, the ideal way to store onions is by stringing them and then hanging the onion string somewhere cool and dry; avoid the kitchen, as it's too humid.

1 Cut a length of string approximately 1.2 m (4 ft) long; don't be tempted to use a longer length or the onion string will be too heavy. Tie a knot at one end of the string to prevent it from fraying, then attach the other end to a firm hook so that the string is hanging down.

2 Take the first onion, hold the bulb and tie the foliage onto the base of the string by enclosing it in a knot, pulling the knot securely against the foliage.

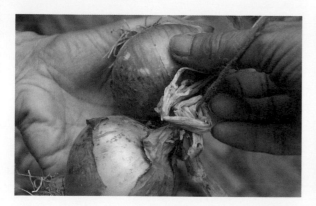

3 Take the second onion, hold the base of the foliage against the string and wrap the foliage around the string 4–6 times. Push the wound foliage gently down on the string towards the onion bulb.

4 Take the next onion, let it rest next to the second onion and wrap the foliage around the string in the opposite direction to the second onion.

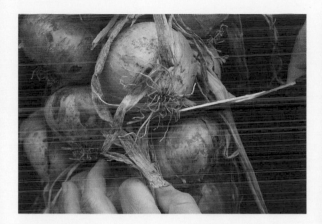

5 Repeat this procedure until you have six or seven rows of onions. You can either trim the stalks to neaten the onion string or leave them hanging loose; it depends on the look you prefer.

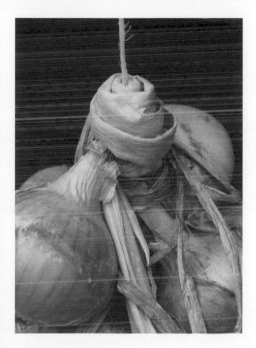

6 If you have a long length of string left at the top, trim it and hang the onion string in your chosen storage space.

Garlic

Surprisingly easy to grow, garlic is an indispensable cooking ingredient. It has been used throughout recorded history for medicinal purposes as well as in cooking and is reputed to be a powerful natural antibiotic and antioxidant.

Garlic is usually planted in autumn, but according to folklore you should plant garlic on the shortest day of the year.

Tips It's not necessary to crop rotate garlic. It grows well with legumes (peas and beans) as a precaution against fungal diseases.

• Birds have a habit of digging up newly planted cloves, so check regularly for the first few weeks and push any disturbed cloves back into the soil.

• Keep some of the bulbs back for planting the following year.

• Don't use cloves for planting that have been bought to eat, as they won't grow in the same way as those specifically designed for planting.

Best varieties Cristo; Solent Wight.

Growing site Sunny and open. Buy a variety that suits your local climate.

Soil Well drained, rich and moisture retentive. Don't plant in freshly manured soil or this can cause plants to rot.

Planting Plant mid-autumn to late winter.

Each clove of garlic planted will produce a new bulb. Split the bulb into individual cloves and plant each clove with the pointed end upwards 2.5 cm (1 in) below the soil surface. Cover with soil so that just their tips are showing through the top. Firm in gently.

Spacing Plant the cloves 10 cm (4 in) apart with 23–30 cm (9–12 in) between rows.

Planting to harvesting 24–36 weeks.

Pests and diseases Birds

Mould: a risk during long, wet spells.

Onion white rot: appears as fluffy white growths on the bulbs. Throw affected bulbs away and avoid growing anything from the onion family on the same site for eight years.

Weeding Garlic's slim foliage means that it doesn't shade out weeds, so keep them at bay by hoeing regularly. Take care not to disturb the bulbs when you are weeding.

Watering Water during spring and summer in dry spells. Don't water once the bulbs are well formed, as it could cause rot.

Harvesting Harvest when the stems have turned to yellow and have bent over. Loosen the soil gently with a fork. Dry the bulbs out in the sun on wire mesh or netting. They must be kept dry, so bring them inside if it rains.

Storing Brush off any excess soil and either make into a garlic string, in the same way as with onions (see pages 92–93), or cut off the stems to store. They can also be stored in a string bag in a dry place. They look wonderful hung in the kitchen.

OPPOSITE AND BELOW: *Garlic is easy to grow and is used by herbalists to treat a wide variety of illnesses.*

Leeks

A member of the onion family, leeks are a versatile vegetable and with a little maintenance are relatively easy to grow. The seedlings need to be transplanted, so some preparation is required before they are placed in their final growing position, but this effort will be rewarded by a plant that can be harvested over a long period of time and one that grows well in cold climates.

Tips Earth up the soil around the stems after the plants have developed, a little at a time in stages.

• Don't allow the soil to get into the crevices of the leaves or this results in it becoming trapped between the layers of the leeks, making them gritty when cooked and eaten.

Best varieties *Autumn Giant2; Carlton AGM; Apollo AGM.*

Growing site A sunny spot that doesn't become waterlogged in the winter months.

Soil Leeks are very happy to grow in any soil, but prefer it to be well drained and firm. Dig in compost or well-rotted manure in the winter. Leave the soil roughly dug through the winter and level off in the spring by raking.

Sowing Sow outdoors in spring when the soil has begun to warm up.

Sow seeds thinly approximately 2.5 cm (1 in) apart in drills about 5 mm (¼ in) deep and cover with fine, sifted soil.

Germination 14–21 days.

Thinning Transplant seedlings when the plants are approximately 20 cm (8 in) high and the stalks the thickness of a pencil. Water the soil where they are going to be planted the day before. Using a thick dibber, make vertical holes 15 cm (6 in) deep

and 15–23 cm (6–9 in) apart, moving the dibber from side to side so that they are slightly larger at the top. Lower each seedling gently into a hole and fill the holes with water. The water will wash enough soil over the base of the plant to allow it to become established. As you weed the soil surrounding the plants from time to time, the holes will steadily fill up with soil. Gradually earth up the soil around the stems as they grow.

Spacing Set the young plants out in rows 30 cm (12 in) apart with approximately 15 cm (6 in) between each plant.

Sowing to harvesting 30 weeks.

Pests and diseases *Leek rust*: orange powdery spots on the leaves of the plant that occur during long damp spells.

Onion fly: the leaves will turn yellow and droop as the fly tunnels into the plant tissue.

White rot: the leaves turn yellow and a grey or white fungus develops at the base.

Leek moth: white streaks appear on the leaves.

White tips: white papery patches appear on the leaves and the tips die back.

Weeding Keep weeds down by hoeing regularly.

Watering Water well during dry spells in the summer, otherwise water only every 10 days or so, depending on the weather in your area.

Harvesting Leeks are tastier when they are small. Lift gently using a fork. They can be left in the ground over the winter months and harvested as required. Trim the leaves and roots and rinse between the layers of the plant to remove any soil before cooking or eating raw.

Storing Leeks can be stored in the refrigerator for up to five days.

OPPOSITE AND BELOW: *Leeks have a tendency to bolt when exposed to optimal temperatures followed by colder temperatures. Try harvesting while they're still small and before the cold weather sets in.*

PUMPKINS AND SQUASHES

This family, known as cucurbits, includes pumpkins, squashes, cucumbers, courgettes and melons. They grow from vines stretching out along the ground or can be trained up the side of trellis or canes. Many have yellow or white flowers and some have hairy, prickly stems.

Winter squashes and pumpkins

The quintessential colour of autumn. Squashes and pumpkins are from the same family as courgettes and share their vine-like stems. They are very exciting to grow – to produce a huge pumpkin from such a tiny seed is a truly magical experience. The plants can take up a lot of room, as the stems will try to stretch out to find space for the flowers and fruits to open out. They also take lots of nutrients from the soil, so grow particularly well if planted directly into compost heaps or manure piles.

Best varieties Pumpkin: *Becky*; *Jack Be Little*; Squash: *Butternut*; *Cobnut*.
Growing site Spacious, sunny spot.

Tips Smaller varieties can be grown on a thick support such as a trellis or arch, which allows the fruit to hang down; if they become too heavy, they can be supported with nets tied to a structure.

• For the best chance of growing the biggest fruits, leave just one fruit on the plant, and when young, put it on a piece of wood or a brick to protect it from pests and keep it off damp soil.

• Apply a liquid fertilizer every few weeks.

• When the fruits have developed, frosts will make the flesh mushy. Place straw or cardboard around the plants to protect them.

Soil Well drained, fertile and moist. Dig in a significant quantity of well-rotted manure or compost before planting.

Sowing Sow indoors around one month before the last frosts. Sow seeds 1 cm (½ in) deep in 7.5-cm (3-in) pots. Transplant outside when the seedlings are large enough to handle and the risk of frosts has passed, hardening off before planting in the ground. If the weather is still cold, cover the plants with a cloche or fleece until the soil warms up.

If planting directly outside, dig an individual hole for each plant approximately 30 cm (12 in) deep and refill the hole with well-rotted manure or compost. Plant three seeds in each hole, 2.5 cm (1 in) deep and 7.5–10 cm (3–4 in) apart. When the shoots have formed, thin out to leave the strongest young plants.

Pinch out growing tips when 30–38 cm (12–15 in) high to stimulate the side shoots.

Germination 5–10 days.

Spacing Thin seedlings to one plant every 46–90 cm (18–36 in).

Sowing to harvesting 10–14 weeks.

Pests and diseases *Powdery mildew*: as with all cucurbits, squashes and pumpkins don't like their leaves being splashed with water, which can cause this problem.

Mice: these can be a threat in the early stages of growing, as they like to eat the seeds.

Weeding Weed regularly.

Watering Mulch plants well and water every week during dry spells. Water around the plants and not directly onto the leaves.

Harvesting The fruits are ready to harvest when the stems start to dry out. Cut the fruits off the plant as required. After cutting, the fruits will need to cure off the plant for around 10 days, preferably in full sun outside. If the weather is poor, bring them indoors into a warm, dry place, preferably a greenhouse or cold frame if you have one.

If you plan to store squashes or pumpkins over the winter, leave them on the plant as long as possible to give them the best chance to fully ripen and develop a tough skin.

Storing If plants have developed a tough skin, they should keep for up to six months. Store in a dry place. They need plenty of air circulation, so don't stack them too high.

BELOW: A golden giant of the vegetable kingdom.

Courgettes

These are the young fruits of marrows. Easy to grow and prolific, courgettes are very popular in the kitchen garden. Both the flowers and fruit are edible and taste best when they are young and small.

Courgettes are well known for producing a glut, as the fruits appear all at once. The average yield is about 15 courgettes per plant.

Tips If your soil is poor, try digging a hole around 15 cm (6 in) deep and mix in well-rotted manure or compost from a grow bag into the soil, refill the hole and plant the seedling.

• In cold summers the fruit may not set, due to inadequate pollination. Try picking the male flowers and scrunch them up, then put them inside the female flowers. The female flowers have little courgettes behind them and the male flowers simply have a stem.

Best varieties   *Gold Rush*: a yellow variety that crops early; *Venus AGM*: a dark green variety that produces abundant fruits.

Growing site   Courgettes need a sunny spot protected from strong winds.

Soil   Well drained, fertile and moist. Courgettes take up a lot of space; however, they also grow well in grow bags in full sun if space is limited and your soil is poor. Dig in well-rotted manure or compost before planting.

Sowing   Mid- to late spring, after the frosts have finished; the seeds won't germinate if it's too cold.

Sow three seeds, 2.5 cm (1 in) deep and several centimetres or a few inches apart. Cover with a cloche to speed up germination. If sowing indoors, place a single seed 1 cm (½ in) deep in a 7.5-cm (3-in) pot. If sowing outside, sow two seeds per station and thin out as soon as possible.

Germination 5–8 days.

Thinning When the seedlings have produced two or three leaves, transfer them to their final growing position. Most households need only a few plants; it's a common mistake to grow too many courgettes and end up with a glut. Discard the weakest plants and cultivate only the strongest of the seedlings.

Spacing Plant seedlings at least 60 cm (2 ft) apart.

Sowing to harvesting 10–14 weeks.

Pests and diseases The small plants are particularly vulnerable to *slugs* and *snails*.

Watering Water young seedlings every day until the plants have established. Never allow the plants to dry out in hot weather and keep the soil moist. Watering is particularly important once the fruits start to form; the more the plants are watered, the more they will thrive. However, if you see a powdery mildew, this means that you are overwatering. Courgettes don't like to be watered onto their leaves.

Harvesting Use a sharp knife and remove the courgette fruits when they are quite small, approximately 10–15 cm (4–6 in) long. If you prefer a larger fruit (marrow), pick when 20–25 cm (8–10 in) long. Pick often to ensure a continuous crop.

Storing The flowers should be picked and eaten straight away.

For the best flavour, eat soon after harvesting. Courgettes can be kept fresh in the refrigerator for only a few days.

OPPOSITE AND BELOW: *The wonderful bright golden flowers of the plant can also be eaten.*

Cucumber

Fresh, crunchy cucumbers are a welcome, refreshing taste of summer. They can be grown either in the greenhouse or outdoors. There are a number of varieties available, from long and slender, as seen in supermarkets, to shorter and prickly. Generally speaking, you can expect 15 fruits per plant.

If growing cucumbers in pots, tie in shoots regularly onto cane supports. Pinch out the growing tip once the plant reaches the top of its support. Sideways shoots can be pinched out when there are two leaves.

Outdoor varieties don't need supports and can be left to trail along the ground.

Tips Cucumbers have both male and female flowers. The female ones have a small cucumber behind them; the male flowers have a thin stem. With greenhouse varieties, remove the male flowers, as fertilized fruits tend to taste bitter. With outdoor varieties, leave the male flowers on the plant.

• If planting outside, the soil needs to be warmed up before planting, as the fruits will rot away if there is a sudden cold spell. It is best to protect outdoor varieties under cloches for a few weeks.

Best varieties Indoor – *Palermo*, *Luxury*: female variety with long fruit; outdoor – *Natsuhikari*: long but spiny and more resilient to the cold; *Masterpiece*: dark skinned; indoor and outdoor – *Burpless Tasty Green*.

Growing site Indoor varieties: grow under glass at approximately 21–27°C (70–80°F); outdoor varieties: place in a warm, sunny spot in moist soil and sheltered from the wind.

Cucumbers also grow well in a grow bag; plant two per bag.

Soil Must be well drained, rich and moist. Feed with tomato fertilizer weekly.

Sowing Heated greenhouse: sow in early spring; unheated greenhouse: late spring; outdoors: early summer. Plant seeds in small pots in moist seed compost in a warm spot. Sow a single seed sideways in a single pot, 1 cm (½ in) deep. When plants are big enough, plant either into the ground or in the greenhouse in at least 10-litre (2-gallon) pots. When planting in pots, support with canes. Allow four to five weeks from sowing to planting.

Germination 3–5 days.

Thinning Thin out when big enough to handle, disturbing the root ball as little as possible.

Spacing Outdoors: sow three seeds in the ground 2.5 cm (1 in) deep. Cover with a cloche until germination has taken hold, then thin out and keep the strongest plant.

Sowing to harvesting Approximately 12 weeks.

Pests and diseases The most common disease is *powdery mildew*, a dusty white covering on the leaves. Discard badly affected plants or treat with a sulphur dust. Check plants regularly for *red spider mite* and *whitefly*.

Watering Cucumbers like a humid environment. Keep the soil moist, but not waterlogged. Dried-out plants will produce bitter-tasting fruits. In the heat of the day, the leaves will naturally wilt. Wet the ground underneath the leaves so that the leaves don't develop powdery mildew.

Harvesting Cut cucumbers when large enough with a sharp knife; they are best cut before the heat of the day for maximum crunchiness. Harvest regularly; if you leave old fruit on the plant, the new ones won't develop. The more you pick, the more the plant will produce.

Storing Cucumbers can be stored in the refrigerator, but are best eaten as fresh as possible.

OPPOSITE AND RIGHT: *A female flower has a little cucumber growing behind it. The male has a stem, which should be removed to avoid bitterness.*

LEAVES

Leaves have shallow roots and grow well either in the ground or in a variety of containers. Whichever kind you're growing, you'll find space between rows of slower-growing vegetables that will give you a good variety of flavour and colour the whole season.

Salad leaves

Lettuce now comes in an exciting range of colours, textures, shapes and tastes – a far cry from the boring salad greens of the past simply used to bulk out the salad bowl. And growing your own lettuce is both easy and quick.

Growing salad leaves works equally well outside in beds or in containers. Once the frosts have passed, plant them directly into the soil, or if you have a greenhouse, start them off in pots or cell trays. When the seedlings emerge, thin them out to leave gaps between the developing plants.

Tips If you choose cut-and-come-again salad leaves, sow the new seeds every couple of weeks to give you a succession of leaves all summer.

• Plan your kitchen garden so that the lettuce will be in the shade of taller plants, such as tomatoes or sweetcorn, in the heat of the summer, to help reduce bolting.

Best varieties Lettuce varieties can be loosely categorized into four groups, each with its own growth and taste characteristics: crisphead, butterhead, leaf and romaine or cos.

You can end up with a glut of leaves, so only sow as much as you need and sow a range of colours and textures to make your salad bowl interesting. Choose some cut-and-come-again varieties where you cut off the leaves as needed

and the plant will continue to produce more leaves all through the summer.

Growing site Salads are usually sown in an open position to make the most of the sunshine, but as it gets warmer, sow in light shade, as salads grown in hot spots are liable to produce bitter leaves.

Soil Lettuce can be grown in a wide range of soils, but loose, fertile, sandy loam soils well supplied with organic matter are best. The soil should be well drained and moist but not soggy. Lettuce does not have an extensive root system, so ensure there is an adequate supply of moisture and nutrients for proper development.

Sowing Grow in the greenhouse from late winter to early spring ready for planting outside as soon as the frosts pass.

Lettuce Seed is very small, so a well-prepared seedbed is essential; large clods of soil will not allow proper seed-to-soil contact. If sowing outside, rake the surface to a fine, crumbly texture. Mark out the row with a garden line and make a drill by creating a long, shallow groove in the soil approximately 1 cm (½ in) deep.

Germination Approximately 7–14 days.

Thinning Wait until the seedlings are 5–8 cm (2–3 in) high, dig a series of small holes and drop the seedlings in.

Spacing Space approximately 15 cm (6 in) apart if sowing narrow varieties or 30 cm (12 in) apart if growing varieties with larger heads.

OPPOSITE: Growing a good variety of leaves will give your salad bowl interesting colours and flavours.

Sowing to harvesting Depends on the variety; check the seed packet for details.

Pests and diseases *Slugs* are the biggest problem, particularly in damp conditions. Sow in cell trays to protect the seedlings from both slug attacks and poor weather.

Weeding An organic mulch will help suppress weeds and keep soil temperatures cool. Pull weeds by hand, taking care not to damage the roots of the plants.

Watering Keep lettuce well watered, as it's prone to bolting if stressed.

Harvesting All lettuce types should be harvested when full size but still young and tender; over-mature lettuce can taste bitter and woody. Leaf lettuce is harvested by removing individual outer leaves so that the centre leaves can continue to grow. Other types can be harvested by removing the outer leaves, digging up the whole plant or cutting the plant about 2.5 cm (1 in) above the soil surface; a second harvest is often possible this way. Crisphead varieties should be picked when the centre is firm.

Storing It's best to eat lettuce as soon as it has been picked. It will, however, keep in a plastic bag in the refrigerator for up to two days.

BELOW: Fresh salad leaves come in an array of different colours and varieties – they don't have to be green.

Swiss chard

This vegetable has highly colourful stems, available in bright pink, red and orange as well as white, and makes an impressive sight in the vegetable bed. It's an especially welcome addition to the kitchen garden in winter when colour is lacking and grows extremely well in containers. An easy vegetable to cultivate, you can cut and come again right through the growing season.

Swiss chard can either be cooked or used raw in salads, and is particularly good when eaten young and tender. The leaves and the stems are best cooked separately because they require different cooking times.

> *Tips* Grow plenty because, like spinach, it cooks down to almost nothing.
>
> • Cut plants regularly to avoid them bolting in warm weather.
>
> • In winter, cover the plants with fleece or a cloche to protect them from bad weather.

Best varieties Bright Lights AGM.
Growing site Open and sunny.
Soil Moist and fertile
Sowing Sow in late spring. Sow seed in a seed tray and transplant seedlings when big enough to handle.

For cut-and-come-again plants, sow seeds directly into the ground in drills approximately 1 cm (½ in) apart.
Spacing Grow in rows 45 cm (18 in) apart.
Germination 10–14 days.
Sowing to harvesting 12 weeks.
Pests and diseases *Slugs* and *snails* will attack young plants.
Weeding Keep weeds down by hoeing or weeding by hand regularly.

RIGHT: Swiss chard comes in a variety of fantastic brightly coloured stalks.

Watering Keep the soil moist during dry spells, but plants can withstand a drought well.
Harvesting Cut plants when the stems and leaves are large. Don't cut too close to the base of the plant; cut approximately 5 cm (2 in) above the base to allow the plant to re-sprout.

Discard the outer leaves if they are damaged and harvest the inner leaves.
Storing Leaves can be frozen for cooking, but if using in salads, eat immediately after picking.

Spinach

Spinach is a very adaptable vegetable, eaten both raw and cooked. It's also easy to grow and, if growing the perpetual type, will keep cropping over a long season.

There are two types of spinach: perpetual and true. Perpetual (winter) spinach is a cut-and-come-again crop, which means that the more you cut it, the more it will grow, resulting in a much longer cropping season. The leaves are generally darker and it has a stronger flavour than true spinach. True (summer) spinach only lasts a limited amount of time; once the plant is cut it will die off, and it often bolts and goes to seed more quickly than the perpetual type. However, the leaves are more tender than perpetual varieties.

Tips Grow lots of spinach, as it cooks down to next to nothing in the pot.

• Cover perpetual spinach with a cloche or straw to protect from cold weather.

Best varieties Perpetual – *Perpetual Spinach*; True – *Emilia*; *Galaxy*.

Growing site Light shade. Grows well as an intercropping plant; try planting it between some tall vegetables that offer a little light shade.

Soil All spinach will grow in almost any soil, but it prefers soil mixed with well-rotted manure or compost.

Sowing Perpetual: early spring to late summer; true: early spring to early autumn.

Both varieties can be started off inside and then transplanted outside as soon as the soil has warmed up and the risk of frost has passed. Plant in drills 2.5 cm (1 in) deep. Water in well.

Germination Perpetual: 2–3 weeks; true: 10–14 days.

Thinning True: thin seedlings to 8 cm (3 in) apart.

Spacing Perpetual: plant at 23-cm (9-in) intervals in rows 45 cm (18 in) apart; true: if planting directly into the ground, plant in rows 30 cm (12 in) apart.

Repeat sowings of true spinach every two to three weeks to provide you with a continuous crop throughout the season.

Sowing to harvesting Perpetual: 12 weeks; true: 10–12 weeks.

Pests and diseases *Slugs*: a common problem, particularly for young shoots.

Birds: they seem to love spinach; if this is a problem, cover with a net.

Weeding Keep weeds down by gently hoeing or weeding by hand around the crops.

Watering Water well, particularly in dry spells. The true variety can easily bolt in hot weather if the plant gets stressed.

Harvesting Pull up alternate plants of true spinach when they are large enough to use and harvest the plants that are left by cutting the leaves when they reach the appropriate size. Cut perpetual spinach to leave a 2.5–5-cm (1–2-in) stump to re-sprout.

Storing Best eaten immediately, but spinach can be stored in a plastic bag in the refrigerator for up to two days.

BELOW: Beautiful crisp green spinach will grow abundantly in most soils.

Oriental vegetables

The demand for these vegetables is increasing as the popularity of oriental cooking expands. Most are grown in the same way as cabbages and lettuces, and some are easy to cultivate. They look attractive, mature fast and many can be harvested through the winter when other vegetables are scarce. They are very tasty and great used in stir-fries, steamed or eaten raw in salads.

Try growing the leafy mustards komatsuna and mizuna, Chinese yams and Chinese cabbage, lablab beans and pak choi.

Sowing and care Oriental vegetables are used to having 12 hours of daylight and 12 hours of darkness and it's recommended that they are sown after the longest day of the year and then thinned in the same spot without transplanting. They grow very fast to produce a heavy crop and can have a tendency to bolt if their roots aren't kept moist or if they are overcrowded.

If sowing in a seedbed, let them grow in situ and thin out if necessary, but avoid root disturbance as much as possible. They can be grown in cell trays and transplanted when large enough to handle, but do so very carefully. Pak choi and other oriental vegetables can also grow very well in grow bags, but you may have to split the bags open at the front to allow them some extra space. Protect late plants from frost with fleece or cloches.

Pests and diseases *Slugs* and *snails* are the two biggest pests. Oriental vegetables often have large leaves and are the ideal environment for pests to hide in. Check the underside of the leaves regularly.

Harvesting Harvest leafy plants as you would cut-and-come-again lettuce (see page 106). Pick when about 10 cm (4 in) in height. Harvest the largest leaves first, allowing the other leaves to come through. Pick Chinese cabbage when immature and stir-fry several young plants together for a delicious vegetable dish.

BELOW LEFT AND RIGHT: Pak choi grows easily, but can be prone to pests hiding inside the layers of leaves.

STEM AND PERENNIAL VEGETABLES

This is a very varied group that includes vegetables such as asparagus, rhubarb (technically a vegetable, rather than a fruit!), sweetcorn and artichokes. Tomatoes are also a perennial vegetable, although they're cultivated as an annual, along with peppers and chillies, as they're not climate hardy. Rhubarb is mostly treated as a fruit and eaten as a delicious dessert.

Asparagus

You need patience to grow asparagus, but the wait is well worth it. You'll also need enough space to set up a separate bed that will be dedicated to the crop over many years. Asparagus takes three to four years to establish, but it then crops for 10–30 years. It's easier and faster if grown from crowns that are one or two years old.

When mature and ready to harvest, these plants will emerge overnight from the ground and are truly a kitchen garden treasure.

Best varieties Franklim (male variety); Grolim (male variety); Jersey Knight (male variety).
Growing site Choose a sheltered and sunny position. Avoid frost pockets and windy positions, as they can damage the fern, reducing the amount of nutrients being stored in the crowns.
Soil Well drained, rich and fertile. Asparagus prefers a sandy soil enriched with plenty of well-rotted manure.
Planting Plant early to mid-spring.

Dig a trench 20 cm (8 in) deep and 30 cm (12 in) wide. Cover the base with 7.5 cm (3 in) of mounded compost or well-rotted manure. Spread the roots over the mound, cover with 5–7.5 cm (2–3 in) of soil and water in well. Gradually fill in the trench as the plants grow; the bed should be level by autumn.

During the first and second autumns after planting, cut the foliage, hoe to create loose soil around the plant and add well-rotted manure. In

Tips When you bring your fleshy crowns home from the nursery or garden centre, plant immediately to avoid the roots from drying out.

• Avoid the soil forming a crust around the plants, which results in bent spears – keep the soil loose.

• Don't allow self-setting seedlings to take hold, as these will inhibit your crop. Buy male varieties, which don't reproduce seedlings; female plants are less productive because they set seeds.

• Only harvest up to midsummer's day.

• Cut down and clear the plants when they turn yellow in autumn. Leave the stumps 2.5–5 cm (1–2 in) above the soil surface.

subsequent years, repeat this procedure, but instead of cutting the foliage, allow the spears to grow and rake off the loose soil in the spring.

Germination 3–4 weeks.

Spacing Set the crowns 45 cm (18 in) apart.

Planting to harvesting 2–3 years.

Pests and diseases *Asparagus beetle*: eats both stems and leaves. Pick off the larvae and any mature beetles, wash plants with a soap solution and remove damaged leaves and stems.

Rust: remove and destroy affected plants.

Slugs: these will occasionally cause damage to emerging spears.

Weeding Keep the growing area free from weeds by hand weeding, taking care not to damage shoots or leaves.

Watering Water only when the plants are young in dry spells, particularly in the first year.

Harvesting Harvest from the third season from mid-spring to midsummer. Cut the spears when they are 15–20 cm (6–8 in) tall with a sharp serrated knife (you can buy special asparagus cutting knives), cutting 5 cm (2 in) below the ground level.

Only take one or two spears from each plant during the first two seasons. In subsequent seasons, harvest as required for up to an eight-week period.

It's essential to cut every spear, as this stimulates the dormant buds in the crown to grow.

Storing Asparagus is at its most delicious when eaten fresh, but the spears also freeze well. To prepare for freezing, remove any grit from the plants and tie into small bundles with string. Blanch for 2–4 minutes before draining, cooling and freezing in a freezerproof container.

You can store the spears for up to a week in the refrigerator.

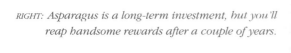

RIGHT: Asparagus is a long-term investment, but you'll reap handsome rewards after a couple of years.

Globe artichokes

This vegetable will bring an element of drama to your kitchen garden. It's a tall, magnificent plant featuring big green heads tinged with purple and will grow to a height of about 1.2 m (4 ft). It's often grown purely as an ornamental plant in a herbaceous border for its architectural form and bright, thistle-like flowers.

Globe artichokes are best when harvested during the second season and they will reach their peak in the third or fourth year. Because of this and the fact that you won't need to rotate them, it's best to allocate them their own growing space in your garden.

Growing globe artichokes is more reliable if they're bought as young plants and put straight into the ground rather than raising them from seed.

Best varieties Green Globe, Purple Globe.

Growing site Full sun. Avoid growing artichokes in a frost pocket or in windy spots, as the plant is not fully hardy.

Soil Rich, well-drained soil with added well-rotted manure or compost. Globe artichoke won't grow in clay soils.

Planting and care Plant any time, but best in mid- to late spring or autumn. Grow each plant in its final growing place 10 cm (4 in) deep. Firm the soil and water in generously.

Protect with fleece during frosts.

Spacing Leave 75 cm (30 in) between plants.

Planting to harvesting 18 months.

Pests and diseases Petal blight: a rare problem, causing brown spots on the head. Remove and burn the affected heads.

Aphids and *slugs* can also be a problem.

Weeding Weed well, particularly during the first year after planting.

Watering Give mature plants water only during dry spells and water young plants daily until the plant has established.

Harvesting Harvest early summer to mid-autumn when the heads are mature but still closed. Cut heads to leave a 5–7.5-cm (2–3-in) stem. Remove the main heads first, then remove the smaller heads later in the season.

During warm spells, the artichoke heads can start to open before you've had a chance to harvest them. Check them regularly and cut as required.

Storing If you don't plan to use the artichoke heads straight away, you can stand the stems in a glass of water in the refrigerator and they will keep for up to a week.

Tips Remove the first heads and crop the second season after planting. If you allow the first heads to develop, they will inhibit growth for the following year.

- Regularly remove offsets – young plants attached to the parent – with a sharp knife in spring, making sure you don't damage the roots. Either plant out offsets immediately to create new plants or put on the compost heap if not needed.

- Plant one or two artichoke plants per year over a four-year period for a succession of well-cropping plants.

- During summer months, loosen the soil around the plant with a hoe. In winter, cut the foliage down to the ground and cover all of the crowns with straw. In the second year, remove the straw and apply well-rotted manure in the spring.

- Mulch around plants in late spring.

- Renew plants every three or four years, or the heads can become tough and woody.

OPPOSITE: Globe artichokes are magnificent plants, they will add a rough beauty to the vegetable bed.

Rhubarb

Rhubarb is often regarded as a fruit, but in fact it's a vegetable that we treat as a fruit. It's a very easy plant to grow and the large green leaves and bright pink stems make it a very attractive plant anywhere in the garden.

It's best grown from root division where the young roots are planted straight into the ground, rather than raising from seed. It also grows well in containers. A very adaptable vegetable, rhubarb can be used to make tarts and pies, crumbles, preserves and wine.

Tips Rhubarb leaves are poisonous. Only eat the stems and dispose of the leaves in the compost.

• Hoe around the plants regularly to avoid the soil from forming a crust.

• Remove any flowering shoots that appear before they set seed, as this will exhaust the crowns and limit their growth.

• Feed with a liquid fertilizer during the summer months.

• Plants can be forced in mid-winter into producing a late winter to early spring crop by using a rhubarb forcer – a tall covering placed over the plant. Purpose-made rhubarb forcers can be bought or you can use a tall bucket. Don't force the same plant again for two years.

• Only eat plants that are from the second year of planting.

Best varieties *Atlanta*; *Giant Winter*.
Growing site Warm and sheltered, but not shady.
Soil Well-drained, rich soil. Rhubarb prefers a well-balanced soil that is neither waterlogged nor too dry, but is very easy to grow in most soils. Enrich the soil with plenty of well-rotted manure or compost in autumn before planting.

Planting Plant from late winter to early spring.

Grow each root separately in a 30-cm (12-in) deep hole wide enough to accommodate the root. Cover the root with a mixture of soil and well-rotted manure and water in well.
Spacing 61 cm (24 in) apart.
Planting to harvesting 15 months.
Pests and diseases Rhubarb doesn't suffer from many pests or diseases.
Weeding Weed around the plant area, taking care not to disturb the root.
Watering Water regularly, particularly during dry spells. Spread a generous layer of well-rotted manure or compost as a mulch around plants and continue to water.
Harvesting Cut the crop from mid-spring to midsummer. Pick by hand: hold the stalk close to the ground and pull upwards with a twisting motion. Always leave at least four stalks on the plant and don't pick after midsummer or they will be woody and tough.

Don't pull new rhubarb plants until at least 12–18 months after planting.
Storing Cut and eat fresh as required. Store in the refrigerator for up to two weeks. Rhubarb also freezes well and there is no need to blanch it first.

BELOW: Rhubarb is a familiar sight in most gardens with its giant leaves and bright red stems.

Tomatoes

These have to be the most popular plant for the garden farmer. Tomatoes are easy to grow and offer many different varieties, from large beef tomatoes for slicing to cherry tomatoes that you can pop straight into your mouth. There are several colours available, from bright red to yellow and orange. There is nothing like the smell and taste of freshly picked tomatoes, evoking the very essence of summer. Tomatoes can be grown inside or outside and also in containers or hanging baskets.

Tips Tomato roots are said to deter squitch grass, also known as couch grass, a type of perennial grass that produces runners under the ground.

- If you have green tomatoes that you want to ripen, put them on a sunny windowsill with an apple and they will quickly ripen.

Best varieties *Sun Gold* (cherry); *Golden Sunrise* (yellow); *Tornado* (red).

Growing site Under cover, outdoors, in hanging baskets or in window boxes. Tomatoes grown in the greenhouse will fruit earlier than outdoor plants. If growing outdoors, choose a sunny, sheltered site, if possible against a sunny wall.

It's always best to check the instructions on the seed packet to see whether you're buying an inside or outside variety.

Avoid planting tomatoes directly into the ground in the same places in which they were grown the previous year.

Soil Tomatoes need fertile soil. They grow best in grow bags or large containers filled with fresh potting compost. If planted in the ground, tomatoes thrive in soil that has been enriched with plenty of organic matter and fertilizer.

Sowing Sowing inside: early to mid-spring; outside: mid-spring to early summer, after the last frosts have passed.

Sow thinly in pots or a seed tray. Cover lightly with a layer of seed compost and position in a warm, light place.

Germination 5–10 days.

Thinning When shoots are big enough to handle, thin into individual pots and keep the compost moist. Plant out young plants when they are approximately 15–23 cm (6–9 in) in height.

Spacing 45 cm (18 in) apart.

Sowing to harvesting Approximately 16 weeks.

Pests and diseases Greenhouse tomatoes are particularly susceptible to *whitefly*, *aphids* and *red spider mite*. Growing basil in the greenhouse can deter whitefly. It's best to disinfect the greenhouse before growing any seeds.

Weeding and care Tomatoes shouldn't need much weeding, particularly if they're in a pot or grow bag, but remove any yellow lower leaves. It's important to pinch out the side shoots and tops to allow the plant to concentrate on growing the fruit.

Watering Tomatoes like an even moisture level, which prevents their skins from splitting, so don't let their soil dry out. Feed them regularly with a seaweed fertilizer, following the manufacturer's instructions.

Harvesting Pick tomatoes when the fruit is fully and evenly coloured. Outdoor varieties may remain green, so bring them inside and place on a sunny windowsill to colour.

Storing Tomatoes are best stored in a cool place, but don't store them in the refrigerator, as they tend to lose their flavour. They should keep for up to five days. Always eat tomatoes at room temperature.

RIGHT: *Regularly pinch out side shoots from tomatoes to allow the plant to concentrate growth in the main stems.*

planting tomatoes in a grow bag

Tomatoes are ready to plant into their permanent position when they are sturdy enough to handle and beginning to form their flowers, about 15–23 cm (6–9 in) tall. Place the grow bag in a warm, sunny position where you intend it to remain, as it's very difficult to move the bag once it's planted with tomatoes.

1 If the grow bag is not already marked, make a mark where the tomatoes will be positioned, approximately 45 cm (18 in) apart. Cut two slits forming a cross into the plastic to expose the compost.

2 Make holes in the compost ready for the plants. Remove each plant gently from its pot and very gently ease the seedlings into the holes in the grow bag, taking care not to damage any roots. Water them in.

3 Make a hole in a corner of the grow bag and place a small pot in the hole. Repeat on the opposite diagonal corner so that you have two little pots facing upwards. These are ideal for feeding and watering the tomatoes, as it avoids disturbing the roots. Fix supports to each plant and secure as they grow.

4 Tomatoes can also be sown directly into the ground inside a greenhouse or put into large plastic pots, at least 10 litres (2 gallons) in capacity. Position somewhere firm and secure or plant directly into the soil. This keeps the roots from spreading out, allowing the water and feed to be concentrated directly into the root system.

Sweetcorn

Sweetcorn is reputed to have been grown and eaten by man (and woman) for over 7,000 years. It's best eaten when freshly harvested, as the sugars of the plant start turning to starch as soon as the cob has been picked and tenderness will be quickly lost. If possible, pick, cook and eat within the hour for the ultimate flavour.

To boil, simply remove the foliage and cook for 7 minutes. Sweetcorn is also delicious cooked on the barbecue; wrap each cob in foil and cook on the barbecue grill for about 10 minutes.

Tips Plant sweetcorn in a block rather than in rows, as they are pollinated by the wind; by planting them close to each other, the male flowers will end up on the female flowers.

• Tap the tassels at the top of each stem when the plants have developed in order to help them pollinate.

• Don't mix varieties, as they cross-pollinate and this causes the kernels to turn starchy.

• Sweetcorn plants grow 0.9–2.4 m (3–8 ft) in height, so if they start to sway in high winds, try earthing them up, which encourages the growth of stabilizing roots. Stake the plants with canes and string if they're looking vulnerable.

• Try making popcorn by leaving the cob on the plant until it dries out. Pick and hang in a dry place for a few weeks. Remove the kernels and fry in a pan of hot oil.

Best varieties *Lark, Swallow, Aztec.*
Growing site Prefers a warm, sunny spot with full sun, but sheltered from the wind. When planting with other vegetables, check the position of the sun so that the tall sweetcorn plants don't shade other plants.

Soil Good drainage and enough humus so that the soil doesn't dry out too quickly.
Sowing Best started off in a greenhouse if possible in mid- to late spring. Sweetcorn hates its roots being disturbed and is an ideal plant for sowing in cardboard tubes that can be planted directly into the ground once the seedlings start to appear and the frosts are over (see page 48). If planting using this method, plant one seed per tube. Each plant produces two cobs.
Germination 10–12 days.
Thinning When the last frosts have passed, plant seedlings directly into the ground. If seedlings are left too close together, yields will be reduced.
Spacing Plant in blocks at least four plants deep and wide. Space plants 35–45 cm (14–18 in) apart.
Sowing to harvesting 14 weeks.
Pests and diseases Sweetcorn are remarkably free from pests and diseases. *Smut balls*, a fungal disease, can appear on the cobs and stems in very hot weather. There is no cure, but if spotted, cut them off and burn them, otherwise they will burst open and release black spores.
Weeding Keep weed free, but take care not to hoe too close to the plant, as roots are near the surface.
Watering Watering is important, both as the young plants are developing and when the kernels are swelling. Watering in between these periods is unnecessary, except in particularly hot weather or warmer climates.
Harvesting Cobs are ready to harvest when the ends turn brown. Test for maturity by peeling back the husk to check if the corn is pale yellow and there is a milky liquid when a kernel is pricked; it's then ready to be picked. Take the stem with one hand and push the cob downwards. You should hear a crack as the cob snaps off from the stem.
Storing Sweetcorn is best picked and eaten straight away. It can be stored for up to two days in a refrigerator, but will lose some of its flavour.

OPPOSITE: *Freshly picked and eaten immediately, home-grown sweetcorn tastes completely different to shop-bought corn.*

Peppers and chillies

Peppers and chillies are staples of many diets throughout the world and are a delight to grow, especially if you have a greenhouse or polytunnel. Both members of the capsicum family, they are cultivated in the same way and many different varieties, shapes and sizes of each are available. They are generally green when young and then develop their bright red, yellow or orange colouring when they ripen.

Chillies range from the very fiery to milder, sweet flavours. Once harvested, they can be dried and used all year round. Chillies need a hot growing temperature and a sunny site. If your local climate is cool, they are best grown in a greenhouse. Chillies are an excellent source of vitamin C, stimulate the circulation and boost the metabolism.

Tips Once the plant is producing fruit, help it along by giving it a small amount of organic liquid fertilizer every few weeks.

• When the plant is around 15 cm (6 in) tall, you can remove the growing tip to encourage the plant to become more bush-like.

• The longer you leave chillies on the plant, the hotter in flavour they will become. Leaving chillies on the plant beyond their readiness for harvest will result in a decline in further yields.

• There are many varieties of chilli to choose from, some hotter than others, so check the seed packets for guidance on the hotness of the fruits.

• Wear rubber gloves when handling hot chillies to protect your hands from the potentially burning membranes and seeds.

• Support plants with canes tied with string to give them extra strength when the fruits form.

Best varieties Chilli – *Jalapeño*: a highly productive plant covered in medium-hot fruits; *Hungarian Hot Wax*: a good plant for cooler climates with fruits that start yellow to green (mild), then ripen to orange and red (hot); peppers – *Gourmet AGM*; *Gypsy AGM*.

Growing site A hot, sunny environment or greenhouse with a good amount of light.

Soil Grow in multi-purpose compost or grow bags. If planting outside, the soil must be well drained and moisture retentive; dig in well-rotted manure before planting.

Sowing Sow in late winter to early spring in the greenhouse or polytunnel.

Sow the seeds of peppers and chillies in small pots. To sow indoors, sow three seeds in each 2.5-cm (1-in) cell of a seedling tray.

Germination 14–30 days.

Thinning When the seedlings have reached approximately 4 cm (1½ in) in height, transfer to individual, approximately 10-litre (2-gallon) pots. If using grow bags, space the plants approximately 25 cm (10 in) apart. Make sure the pots have plenty of good drainage.

Sowing to harvesting 18 weeks.

Pests and diseases *Red spider mite*; *aphids*; *whitefly*.

Watering Mist the plants regularly to reduce the risk of red spider mite. Water regularly, but take care not to waterlog. Water two or three times a week; overwatering will cause the roots to rot.

Harvesting Pick fruits when they are swollen and glossy. Chillies and peppers take a few weeks to develop and will take a further couple of weeks to change from green to red. They can be harvested either green or red. The green fruits of chillies tend to be milder than the red. They'll begin to shrivel after they've been on the plant for a while, but can still be harvested and used at this stage.

If picking peppers when they're green, place under glass or on a windowsill and they'll turn red in about three weeks.

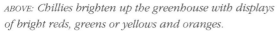

ABOVE: Chillies brighten up the greenhouse with displays of bright reds, greens or yellows and oranges.

ABOVE: Plump red or green peppers taste crisp and juicy straight from the plant.

Cut the fruits with a knife to avoid damaging the stems.

Storing Peppers will keep in a plastic bag in the refrigerator for up to two weeks.

Chillies can be left to dry and used all year round. Try tying them up with string and hanging from a hook in the kitchen – this is known as a rista of chillies.

Fresh chillies can be stored for up to two weeks in a ventilated plastic bag in the refrigerator. Chilling affects the flavour, so bring them to room temperature before use.

GROWING FRUIT

Fruit can be grown in every garden, no matter what the size of your plot. While a separate fruit garden is ideal if you have the space, you don't need a room-sized fruit cage to be able to grow fruit. Some fruits grow well in containers and will only take up as much space as a rose bush. In any case, choose what types of fruit to grow according to your tastes.

There are so many varieties to choose from, and bear in mind that the shop-bought ones will taste very different to home-grown fruit, so it's best to test out which you prefer by visiting a fruit-picking farm, friends or allotment holders and enjoy having tasting sessions before choosing which plants to grow.

Once established, a fruit garden is much less effort to maintain than a vegetable garden. When starting out, check that the variety you have chosen is suited to your soil, local climate and the space you have available to avoid potential problems. When harvesting fruit, choose a dry day and never shake or throw things at the tree or plant to make the fruit fall off. Fallen fruit will bruise and therefore be wasted.

Fruit falls into two main categories:

Tree fruit

These are the largest fruit plants and live the longest. They include apples, pears and plums, and come in a range of varieties, from full-sized to dwarf plants. They usually have just one main stem and adopt a tree form. It can take a few years for the tree to start fruiting, but once it has become established, it will last longer and have higher yields than soft fruits.

Most fruit trees prefer to have other fruit tree companions so that they can cross-pollinate each other, although it's possible for some single fruit trees to be self-fertile. In order to cross-pollinate, the trees must be in the same family group. For example, a pear tree can't cross-pollinate with apples and so on. You need at least two varieties of each species of the fruit tree you plant. The trees are cross-pollinated by insects, mostly bees, when the trees are blossoming. If you have only a single tree, you can borrow branches from another tree. Find a friendly neighbour with the same type of tree and ask them if you can cut a couple of branches off. Simply cut the branches when the tree is in blossom and bring them home, then put them in a bucket of water and place them under your tree. The bees will do the work of cross-pollinating from there on for you.

Soft fruits

This group includes all berries and currants. These plants are perennials, but they often need renewing every few years to produce the best crops. Raspberries and currants need replacing about every seven years and strawberries every three or four years to prevent yields being affected by viruses and other disorders. They will often need some sort of support using canes, wires or poles, which saves space, increases yields and

OPPOSITE: With so many varieties of apple to choose from, enjoy a few tasting sessions before deciding which one to grow.

takes the weight of the developing fruit. They tend to be attacked from birds more than tree fruit and therefore may need increased protection using netting or net cages.

Preparing a site

When preparing your fruit-planting area, make sure you choose a sunny yet sheltered site. Fruits need sun to mature and ripen the stems that bear the fruiting buds, although some will tolerate a little shade. All fruits prefer a well-draining soil and the flowers will need protection from frosts and cold winds. Depending on your site, you may need to build natural or erected screens, but ensure that they don't cast too much shade directly onto the plants.

Add plenty of well-rotted manure or compost when preparing the planting area and mulch young plants during dry spells to prevent them drying out. Before planting, soak bare roots in a bucket of water for a few hours to give them a good start.

BELOW: Fruit cages can be bought and easily erected to protect fruit from unwanted attacks from birds and pests.

Pruning pointers

Many of us are familiar with wild fruit growing in hedgerows and fields, and fruits will grow abundantly when left to their own devices, but when growing in your garden, pruning will redirect growth and limit the size of your plant to fit into its allotted space. Cultivated fruit will generally yield larger fruit than if left to grow wild.

The top bud on a pruned stem usually grows first and in the direction that it points towards. When pruning, choose which direction you want your plant to grow in. This is useful when growing along trellises or wires.

As a guide, prune summer side shoots to five leaves and in winter prune to two buds, always cutting above a bud. Young, green stems are easier to train because they are soft and more pliable. Take care when training old stems, as they can be brittle and break off.

When pruning trees, cuts must be clean; pare off any ragged pieces and use only sharp secateurs. Press with a downward motion. It's normal to make some wrong cuts, and as a result, snags of dead wood will form, so cut these pieces off as they develop. Paint tree-pruning cuts with a shop-bought natural resin – choose one that's suitable for organic gardening – to seal and heal them and to protect the tree from diseases and harmful pests. It will also give some protection against frosts.

Keeping fruit in trim

There are a few basic tools that are needed for pruning your fruit:

    Pruning knife
    Long-handled pruner
    Two-bladed secateurs
    Pruning saw

Keep pruning tools sharp, and if pruning diseased stems, sterilize tools after use to avoid contaminating other plants.

fruit-growing frameworks

There are a variety of different decorative shapes that you can create with your fruit plants through pruning, which can save space and increase yields.

Fans Most varieties of fruit are suitable for fan training, though avoid tip-bearing apples and pears, and they work well on south-facing walls. They consist of a short, clear stem approximately 45 cm (18 in) in length with the branches above arranged to form a fan shape. The fan needs horizontal wires for support. Train a one-year-old tree using canes tied to wires 15 cm (6 in) apart.

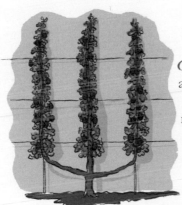

Cordons Young fruit trees can be trained up a fence, either upright or at an angle, with one stem and no long laterals. Angle cordons make picking easier. Use a one-year-old plant with a single, strong leading shoot.

Espaliers Here, wires are stretched horizontally 30 cm (12 in) apart between posts and a central stem trained to grow vertically, with the lateral shoots tied at 90 degrees to canes fastened to the wires.

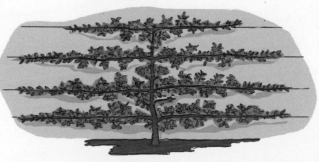

Apples

The most useful fruit for cooler climates, there are thousands of varieties of apple available; choose one that suits your taste and local climate. They will grow well in most soils, though they prefer not to grow in a limy soil.

Planting   Planting will depend on the variety; plant bare-rooted trees in the autumn and container-grown trees at any time of the year. Prepare the planting area by clearing any surrounding weeds and mix in plenty of well-rotted manure or compost. When planting, the soil mark on the stem should be level with the soil and the roots spread out evenly in the dug-out hole. Refill the hole with soil mixed with well-rotted manure or compost.

Weed the area where the tree will be planted and keep the area near the trunk free from both weeds and grass.

Young trees will need support as soon as they are planted. Provide horizontal wires for cordons and espaliers (see page 125) before planting. Water young trees during dry spells and mulch them well.

Pruning   During the first four years, the purpose of pruning is to train the branches into a framework for providing good cropping for future years. Prune to provide an open centre and a cup-shaped tree. Remove dead or weak twigs and branches.

Harvesting Large trees will start cropping between four and six years and dwarf varieties crop around two years after planting. Pick apples when they are in their peak condition.

LEFT: *Apples glistening in the morning dew, ripe and ready to be harvested.*

Pears

These prefer slightly warmer conditions than apples and blossom slightly earlier, but are grown in very similar ways and like the same soil conditions.

Heavy crops can cause branches to break. Support fruit-filled branches by propping them up with a tall pole and attach strong rope tied from the centre of the branch to the top of the pole.

Planting As with apples, planting will depend on the variety; plant bare-rooted trees in the autumn and container-grown trees at any time of the year. Prepare the planting area by clearing any surrounding weeds and mix in plenty of well-rotted manure or compost. Young trees will need support as soon as they're planted. Water young trees during dry spells and mulch well.

Pruning Pear trees require lots of training during their first four years of life to create the basic framework needed to produce a good crop in later years. Branches need to be cut back severely in order to create an open-centred tree. After four years they will need only maintenance pruning by cutting out dead wood. Prune cordons and espaliers as well as dwarf varieties in summer to inhibit shoot growth.

Harvesting When the fruits pick easily from the tree, they're ready to harvest. Some varieties can be picked to ripen in store. Store on shelves or in boxes in a cool place until ready to eat. Bring them inside in a warm place when ready to eat and they will soften.

RIGHT: *Pears are an adaptable, juicy fruit and are easy to grow.*

Cherries

These delicious fruits are very popular with the bird population. Consequently, to ensure a successful crop, they'll need to be grown under a netting frame.

Planting Cherries will tolerate either full sun or a shady position. Water regularly in dry spells. Keep the moisture levels regular, as heavy, irregular watering can split the fruits. If planting in dry soils, water regularly while the fruits are developing to prevent them splitting.

Pruning Prune in spring and summer. Cut out fruited shoots after harvesting, then in the following spring, thin out young shoots to leave an equivalent number of replacements to bear a new crop.

Harvesting Pick fruits with their stems on as soon as they're ripe.

Plums

Choose the highest spot in the garden and a position that has lots of sun for the best crop. Birds will devour any buds and fruits from plum trees, so they'll benefit from some netting protection. Water in dry spells. Keep moisture levels regular, otherwise the fruits can split. Hoe to keep down weeds at the base of the tree, taking care not to damage young roots.

Heavy crops can cause branches to break. Support fruit-filled branches by propping them up with a tall pole and attach strong rope tied from the centre of the branch to the top of the pole.

Planting Plant in a moisture-retentive and well-drained soil in the autumn and stake young plants for the first five to six years.

Pruning Prune branches of a two- or three-year-old tree in early spring. Aim for three to five strong branches at the two-year-old stage, with the branches as horizontal as possible. At the three-year-old stage, eight strong branches should be established with several minor branches spaced around the tree. In the case of an established tree, prune in late spring or early summer. Pruning at this stage should be for maintenance only and to reduce overcrowding.

Harvesting Harvest the fruits when they pick easily from the tree; the stem will usually remain on the tree.

OPPOSITE AND ABOVE: *Plums come in a variety of wonderful colours. All are sweet and juicy, and are tempting snacks. They also make fantastic preserves and sauces.*

Raspberries

Raspberry plants can be productive for eight to twelve years, and the cropping period during the summer season can last from three to six weeks. They thrive in cool, damp summers, making them the perfect fruit for cooler areas. There are early-summer and autumn varieties, with the latter being a little sweeter. Plant the summer varieties in late summer to early autumn and the autumn varieties at the beginning of the spring.

Raspberries are notorious for producing side shoots that travel underground and they can pop up anywhere in the vicinity of the main row. Keep an eye out for these shoots appearing and chop them off at root level with a spade.

Use netting to protect the fruits from birds.

Planting Raspberries like a well-drained soil that doesn't become waterlogged. They need a form of support; use canes, or a post and wire fence. Find a sheltered spot and avoid windy sites, as the plants can be damaged by high winds. They are happier in a sunny spot, but they'll also tolerate slight shade.

Remove all weeds from the growing site and plant a hole big enough for the roots to spread evenly. Cover with a mixture of soil and well-rotted manure or compost. Water plants regularly, particularly young plants and when fruiting.

Pruning Let the first canes grow, but cut the first shoots down before they flower. The second-season canes will then fruit. At the end of the season, cut out the old wood and leave the new shoots to grow for next year.

Harvesting Pick the fruits when they're a raspberry pink and still firm to the touch. Pull the fruit gently away from the plant, leaving the plug behind. Don't harvest on wet days, otherwise the fruit will have a tendency to rot.

LEFT: *Raspberries are sweet and tender and ready to pick when they are a rich 'raspberry' pink.*

Redcurrants and white currants

These fruits are produced on the stubby side shoots of the main branches of a bush. Currants are best grown in a fruit cage if possible, as birds will attack and devour the fruits. If this isn't possible, cover the plants in netting.

Weed by hand; hoeing can damage the roots close to the surface, which encourages the suckers. Suckers should be removed from the roots after the fruiting season. Water thoroughly, particularly when the fruits are emerging.

Planting   Buy two-year-old plants from your supplier. The bush should be short, stout and with four evenly spaced branches.

Plant bare-rooted bushes in late autumn or leave until early spring if this isn't possible. Plant container bushes at any time of year.

Plant in sun or semi-shade in a sheltered spot. Wild redcurrants and white currants will often be found in the dappled sunlight of woodland in northern temperate regions. They are happy to grow in most soils, but prefer well drained soil. Before planting, remove all weeds from the growing site, add a thick layer of well-rotted manure or compost and mix with the soil. Make a hole big enough for the roots to spread out evenly and firmly cover with the mixture of well-rotted manure and soil. Water in well.

Pruning   Pruning every winter will encourage an abundance of fruiting spurs. Cut back new growth by half the size on the main branches and reduce the side shoots to stop them from inhibiting the main branches. Cut out any dead or diseased wood and prevent overcrowding at the centre of the bush.

Harvesting When the fruits are shiny, they're ready to harvest. Once they've gone a dull colour, they are overripe.

RIGHT: *Sharp and tangy, redcurrants will stimulate the taste buds; they make a delicious jelly.*

Strawberries

These are the most popular soft fruits. They're very easy to grow either in the vegetable plot or in containers. Plants produce the best crop after two years and usually last three to four years, after which they will need replacing to produce the best crops. The large-fruited varieties produce runners bearing young plants, which can be planted into the soil to produce more new plants.

Planting They prefer a sunny, sheltered site, but will tolerate a little shade. Good drainage is necessary and well-rotted manure or compost should be added to the soil. Plant little plants during late summer and transplant them 30 cm (12 in) apart in rows 45 cm (18 in) apart. Dig a large enough hole to spread the roots out evenly and make sure that the crown is level with the soil. Cover with soil and water well. Keep strawberry beds free from weeds, as they can inhibit the growth of the plants. If planting in containers, plant at any time. After producing fruit, the plants send out new shoots and little plants start to develop along them. These can be secured into the soil or compost and allowed to grow roots. When they have rooted, separate them from the main plant and replant them.

To protect from frosts, cover plants with fleece or a cloche. Use straw as a mulch, which also serves to rest the fruit and keep it off the moist soil. Water all plants during a dry spell. Keep water off the plants by watering in the morning so that they have a chance to dry out before the night.

Use netting to protect the fruits from birds.

Pruning Straight after harvesting when all the fruits have been picked, cut off all the leaves to approximately 7.5 cm (3 in) above the ground.

Harvesting Pick the fruits when they're red and shiny. Harvest them frequently to encourage new fruit to develop.

LEFT: Bright red strawberries to make strawberry jam, or just to eat as picked with cream or natural Greek yoghurt.

planting strawberries in a box

Strawberries grow very well in containers. If you plant in an old wooden fruit box the colour of the bright red strawberries against the rustic brown box makes a very attractive addition to the garden or as a lovely gift. The moss is used decoratively and pushed into the outside gaps of the box to cover up the black plastic that holds in the compost.

1 Line the box to contain the compost. Try recycling a used plastic compost bag by cutting it up and lining the inside of the fruit box. Cut holes in several places in the base.

2 For drainages, either add some broken pieces of terracotta pots, or recycle a polystyrene plant holder by breaking it into small pieces and distribute evenly in the base of the box.

3 Fill the box generously with a good quality, moisture-retaining compost.

4 Plant 6–8 strawberry plants evenly and water in.

5 Tear off pieces of moss and push into the gaps at the side to cover the black plastic. Place in a warm, sunny position and wait for the fruit to grow.

6 When the fruits begin to emerge, add some clean straw at the base of the plant. This holds the strawberries' weight and acts as a mulch to keep soil temperatures down and deter weeds.

GROWING HERBS

Herbs are as essential as vegetables in the kitchen garden. As well as complementing your vegetable crops in cooking, they can also be used for both therapeutic and cosmetic purposes, such as in health-promoting teas, scented soaps and soothing hand creams.

Taste the difference

Freshly gathered, herbs have a far superior aroma and flavour to their shop-bought equivalents, and because of this, you'll need to use less than specified in the recipe. I made the mistake recently of adding to a favourite risotto recipe the same amount of my freshly picked parsley as I had commercially grown parsley in the past and I completely ruined the dish, as the parsley overwhelmed all the other flavours.

Which herbs?

The choices are bewildering when deciding which herbs to grow, since there are so many varieties of different species to choose from. The best solution is to start off by growing a basic collection of herbs and then experiment over time with other varieties.

How and where to grow

Grow herbs from seed in seed or cell trays under cover and then transplant outside, or plant seeds directly in the ground.

Herb seeds or seedlings can either be dispersed between rows of vegetables or allocated their own spot in the kitchen garden. They usually work well in a space near the kitchen so that you don't have too far to walk when you have a pan sizzling on the hob waiting for its herbal ingredient. They don't usually thrive in an acid soil; they like well-drained soil in a sheltered and sunny spot. Don't add manure to herbs, but instead add some compost or leaf mould. Clear weeds from the herb garden as soon as they appear.

Harvest leaves and shoot tips regularly. This keeps the plants in shape and prevents them going to seed. It also encourages new, fresh growth.

BELOW: Grow a selection of herbs that best suits your needs.

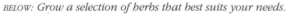

Basil

How to use This popular herb is grown for its strong, aromatic fragrance and flavour, and sweet basil is the most common variety. Eaten both raw and cooked, its leaves are great in salads and pasta and other dishes.

Growing guidelines Grow outside or inside depending on your local weather conditions. Basil is a warm-climate plant, so it prefers a moist soil, and is best sown in early spring (inside) or during late spring (outside, when the weather has warmed up).

When the seedlings have begun to grow, they will need thinning out into larger, approximately 13-cm (5-in) pots, around five seedlings per pot. When they've grown too big for the pots, transplant them into bigger containers. Choose the strongest-looking seedlings when thinning out, but don't throw away the excess – use them in your cooking to add fresh flavour.

When transplanting outside, plant 15–20 cm (6–8 in) apart in full sun. When the basil plants start to flower, cut out the flowers or simply pinch them out to encourage more leaf growth and to preserve the plant's flavour. When harvesting, pick out the top leaves first and don't harvest all the leaves from the plant.

Bay

How to use The glossy leaves of this attractive, moderately hardy small tree or shrub can be picked all year round and used fresh in cooking – they are one of the standard components of a bouquet garni. Alternatively, you can dry bay leaves for storing in an airtight jar for future use by leaving them in a cool, dry and dark place.

Growing guidelines Plant out small plants in autumn or spring. The leaves benefit from being washed with a mist spray to keep them clean. Bay can be grown as a container plant, which gives it some protection in colder climates. Bring containers inside during the winter months in cold regions to protect them.

Chives

How to use These herbs add a decorative element to the herb garden, and their bulbous purple heads are a big attraction for bees. They're a member of the allium family and will add a subtle flavour similar to onion and garlic to your dishes. You can use both the flowers and stems as needed.

Growing guidelines Chives are available as small plants or bulbils. They can also be raised from seed if sown in spring. Plant 23 cm (9 in) apart in sun or light shade.

BELOW: *Basil grown in the greenhouse can deter whitefly.*

BELOW: *Add chive flowers to salads by removing the stem and breaking the florets over the salad.*

Coriander

How to use This plant is grown for both its distinctively flavoured, delicate leaves and its aromatic, lemony-tasting seeds; their flavours are quite different. Coriander leaves (and the roots, which are more intensely flavoured) are highly popular in Chinese and Thai dishes as well as in Indian cooking, which also often features coriander seed, either ground or whole.

Growing guidelines Check the seed packet carefully in order to buy the variety – leaf or seed – that is appropriate to your needs. For leaf varieties: sow straight into the soil in mid-spring and thin to 23 cm (9 in) apart. Crops can be sown at five- to six-week intervals until early autumn. Harvest when plants are 15 cm (6 in) tall and leave to re-grow. For seed varieties: sow straight into the soil in mid-spring and thin to 5 cm (2 in) apart. Harvest the seeds in late summer just before they're ripe and put the seed heads in a paper bag to dry.

Fennel

How to use The feathery leaves of this tall ornamental perennial that attracts friendly insects have a sweet aniseed flavour, as do the seeds, which can be used ground or whole in fish and other savoury dishes.

Growing guidelines Sow early to mid-spring from seed and transplant 60 cm (24 in) apart in well-drained soil in full sun. It can grow to a height of 1.5–1.8 m (5–6 ft). Fennel plants benefit from being divided every three to four years. Pick the leaves in summer as required, and collect the seeds during the late summer period.

Mint

How to use Mint has many different culinary uses, but it's especially valuable for enhancing the flavour of your other vegetable crops, such as freshly dug new potatoes and tender young peas and beans. It's also great for making refreshing and theraputic teas.

BELOW: Fennel has attractive fern leaves and beautiful yellow flowers.

BELOW: Mint is eager to please and will grow abundantly.

Growing guidelines Mint grows abundantly and can all too easily take over the space of other plants and herbs. To prevent it from being invasive, grow in pots and then transplant the whole pot into the ground to confine the roots. Harvest the leaves and shoot tips as required. Trim the stems to ground level in midsummer for fresh supplies in autumn.

Parsley

How to use Probably the most widely used culinary herb, parsley adds its fresh, aromatic flavour to sauces, soups and salads. The flat-leaved variety, as opposed to curly-leaved, is the parsley of choice for Mediterranean dishes.

Growing guidelines You can grow curly-leaved and flat-leaved varieties from seed in early spring to midsummer in situ in moist, rich soil. Parsley likes either dappled shade or full sun. Thin seedlings to 15 cm (6 in) apart, and water well in dry spells. Harvest stems and leaves as required.

Rosemary

How to use This evergreen shrub has aromatic needle-like leaves with a strong taste, which can be used to flavour meat, especially lamb, poultry and game, as well as roasted vegetables and homemade breads.

Growing guidelines Rosemary will grow in abundance anywhere, but prefers well-drained soil in a sunny position.

It's usually propagated by cuttings rather than grown by seed. Snip a 5-cm (2-in) cutting from the new growth of an established plant, remove the leaves from the bottom and dip the tip into a rooting hormone. Place the dipped end into a container of dampened seed compost, position in a warm spot and mist the cutting with a water spray daily. Once the roots have set, transplant into individual pots or plant outside and pinch off the top of the cutting to encourage the branches to develop. Once the plant has matured, pick the stems and use as required.

BELOW: Curly and flat-leaved parsley grow well in containers.

BELOW: Rosemary makes excellent ground cover.

Sage

How to use   This hardy evergreen shrub has long, green/grey or purple, highly aromatic leaves that have one of the strongest tastes of any herb, traditionally used to flavour pork and stuffings.

Growing guidelines   Sow in pots in spring and transplant 60 cm (24 in) apart in sunny and well-drained soil. Pinch out the growing tips to encourage a bushy growth and trim after the plant has flowered. Replace the plants every four to five years. The leaves can be gathered for use as required.

Sorrel

How to use   The broad-leaved variety has a sharp, lemony flavour and is often cooked and eaten in the same way as spinach. It's also delicious chopped up in salads. Use the juice of the leaf to remove rust, mould and ink stains from linen, wicker and silver. Sorrel is also a good dye plant, making a yellow or green dye.

Growing guidelines   Sorrel likes acid soil that retains moisture. Preferably grow in full sun. Sow seeds in spring and divide broad-leaved sorrel every other year in autumn, in order to retain the succulent leaves.

Tarragon

How to use   This perennial herb has narrow, pointed, dark green leaves with an intense, aniseed-type flavour, used in poultry, egg and cheese dishes, and to make tarragon vinegar for salad dressings.

Growing guidelines This herb has wide-spreading, invasive roots. Sow in mid- to late spring in pots and then transplant the whole pot into the ground to avoid it taking over the herb bed. Space 30 cm (12 in) apart in a small group in a warm position with well-draining soil. Pick as required in early to late summer, using the upper sprigs to encourage new growth.

BELOW: *Purple sage has large leaves with a velvety texture.*

BELOW: *Sorrel resembles spinach and is sometimes known as 'spinach dock'.*

Thyme

How to use A member of the mint family, thyme is a short-lived, woody perennial shrub with small, aromatic, greyish-green leaves and is used as a condiment; thyme leaves can be used fresh or dried, as whole sprigs or chopped. Thyme works well as flavouring for all kinds of meat, poultry, fish and vegetable dishes.

There are many different varieties available, but common or garden thyme is the most popular, although lemon thyme, with its citrus tang, is also a good choice.

Growing guidelines Thyme is best bought as young plants. Plant in mid- to late spring 23 cm (9 in) apart in well-drained soil in a sunny position. Harvest the young stems by pulling or cutting from the strong clump. Renew your thyme plants every four to five years.

Thyme can be very woody, but it's not necessary to strip the leaves from the woody twigs,

Tips Use freshly picked herbs with caution, as they are much stronger than shop-bought varieties.

• There are so many variations of each herb to choose from – have fun testing some out before deciding which ones to plant.

• Herbs work very well as tea infusions. Simply pour over hot water and allow the picked herbs to infuse into the water. Remove the stalks and leaves before drinking.

as these are also very aromatic. Simply chop the twigs and leaves up very finely or add to the dish as directed.

BELOW: *Thyme has tiny leaves and a woody stalk; chop the whole stalk and leaves together and add to your ingredients.*

WILD FOOD

Gathering wild food, often available in abundance, is arguably as equally satisfying as growing and picking your own fruit and vegetables. Foraging the hedgerows, woods and fields in your local area and returning to the kitchen to make something fresh is a great way to spend the weekend, and introducing children to the concept of searching for hidden nuts, leaves and berries is all the more exciting because it's a cost-free source of food.

What wild food you can harvest all depends on the nature of your locality, so it's best to find out what people in your local community have eaten from the hedgerows and other areas accessible to the public. I'm not covering wild mushrooms in this section, of which there are many, since you need to be absolutely certain about identifying which ones are safe to eat, otherwise the consequences could be fatal.

Many people regard summer and autumn as the best time for foraging, but in fact summer can be a little scarce for wild food. Spring is an excellent time for gathering, for example, the tips of leaves of the silver birch and the hawthorn bush, which are very tasty when mixed in with other salad leaves. Or try picking goosegrass (cleavers/ *Galium aparine*) in late summer to autumn, whose sticky seeds can be dried out and then ground, roasted and used as a substitute for coffee beans.

When foraging, find areas that are not too close to the road to avoid contamination from pollution, which enters the soil that feeds the plants. If you venture onto someone else's land, remember to ask permission before you forage. Footpaths often run through farmers' fields, but the wild food will be theirs and not yours.

OPPOSITE: Check out the wild food in your local area – you never know what exciting surprises there will be in the hedgerows and bushes around you.

Here are some common wild foods to look for:

Rosehips

These are the seed pods of roses. In the garden, roses are mostly pruned and trimmed before the rosehips have had time to develop, but they grow abundantly in the wild. These small, berry-sized, reddish seed balls left on the tips of the stems are best picked after the first frosts.

There was a great tradition in post-war England of foraging rosehips, when the government would officially give schools time off to pick them from the hedgerows. The fruits were then collected centrally, processed at a depot and made into syrup, which was redistributed back to the schools to provide the schoolchildren with an invaluable source of vitamin C. It was recorded that in one year they picked 7,500 kg (148 hundredweights)!

Crab apples

These little wild apples are very bitter when eaten raw, but they make delicious preserves, such as crab apple jelly.

Blackberries

These are possibly the most well-known wild fruit. It's a tradition with many families to go on a blackberry hunt in early autumn when fruits are dripping from their prickly bushes and return to make blackberry and apple crumble or bramble jelly.

Hazelnuts

If you can get to them before the squirrels, these nuts can be eaten right off the bush, or collect a bunch and let them dry for a few days until they can be easily freed from their sheathing. They are reputed to have aphrodisiac properties.

Wild garlic

The pungent aroma of woodland lush with beautiful green leaves bearing little white, fluffy heads of flowers means that spring is in full swing. They often grow together with bluebells – a truly magical sight. You can use the whole plant in salads or just the leaves as you would spinach.

Wild sorrel

This is a herb with a pronounced lemony flavour that can be cooked in the same way as spinach. As with most foraged leaves when using raw, it's best to tear or chop them up and mix in with other salad leaves to add a tangy edge, rather than eating them on their own.

Dandelion

This grows in most lawns, so you won't have far to go. The time to harvest dandelion leaves is early in the spring, when they are at their youngest and before they flower. Young dandelion leaves are tender and delicious served raw in salads or sandwiches. Dandelion root can be ground and used as a substitute for coffee, and dandelion flowers can be used both as an ingredient and for garnishing dishes.

Elderflower and elderberries

A very versatile plant, both the flowers and berries make excellent wines. The berries can be cooked with other fruits to enhance their flavour and made into relishes, sauces, cordials, jellies and jams.

LEFT: Wild garlic is always a feast for the senses.
RIGHT: Be sure to wear gloves when foraging as nettle stings and thorns may soon find their way into your hands.

Nettles

There aren't many hedgerows – or gardens – without nettles, and you can use them to make delicious soups and health-giving teas, as well as a liquid feed for your plants (see page 50). Don't touch fresh nettles with your bare hands; use gloves or tongs to move them around to avoid being stung. Cook the nettles until they're completely soggy or wilted to deactivate the sting before eating. When foraging for nettles, pick only the top 10 cm (4 in) of the plant, as the thick stems are too woody to eat. When cooking, they mix well with other greens such as spinach, chard or kale.

Sloes

These are the damson-like fruits of the blackthorn bush, which often makes up part of a hedgerow, or grows near the edge of a field. Even if you live in an urban environment, you'll likely to find sloes growing in parks and on scrubland. They're best picked after the first frosts. Too tart to eat raw, they are most famously combined with gin and sugar to make sloe gin, but they can also be used to make jams, jellies and sloe cheese or to flavour vinegar or make wine.

STORING PRODUCE

Vegetables and fruits are mostly best left on the plant or tree until they are ripe, and then picked and eaten straight away. But sometimes a plant might crop all at once, giving you too much produce. Courgettes typically produce a 'glut' in this way, and if you leave them on the plant, they grow into huge marrows that can be large enough to feed a family of 20. In any case, this vegetable is much tastier when small and young, so if you have lots of courgettes, make them into chutneys, which you can store, or cook them up in risottos and even cakes.

Many vegetables will keep for some time in the refrigerator in a plastic bag, and some can be successfully frozen, but freezing isn't suitable for all crops. I have given specific storage tips for each type of vegetable (see pages 64–121), but the following are some general guidelines on storing different kinds of produce.

Bulbs and chillies

Onions and garlic store very well if either plaited together or strung and hung in a dry place (see pages 92–93). Chillies can either be strung together using a strong thread or string, called a rista of chillies, and then hung up to dry, or dried out and then kept in airtight jars for use all through the winter months.

Root vegetables

Potatoes store well in hessian or paper sacks, but if exposed to light when stored, they will turn green and poisonous. Partially green potatoes are safe to use if you cut off the green parts entirely. If storing in paper sacks, leave the sack slightly open to allow the moisture to escape. Make sure you store potatoes somewhere cool, but they shouldn't be frozen or kept in plastic bags.

If you have a well-drained soil, carrots and parsnips can be left in it over winter to harvest on demand. They benefit from some protection with cloches or fleece when the weather is very cold. Leaving them in the ground increases the risk of insect damage and digging them up when the ground is frozen is a little tricky.

Root veg can be stored in layers of sand in boxes. Cut off the foliage of parsnips and carrots and tear the foliage of beetroots to 1 cm (½ in) above the top of the root. Brush off any excess soil before layering them with the dry sand in the boxes, making sure they're not touching one another.

Tip When storing vegetables and fruit in the short term, show off your produce. Collect pretty baskets, wooden boxes and attractive containers, and enjoy displaying your harvest on shelves and tabletops in your kitchen.

OPPOSITE AND RIGHT: Display produce in baskets and in your kitchen. It may encourage others to share in your passion.

Pumpkins and winter squashes

Harden the shells of the produce by keeping them at room temperature for two weeks, then store at 7–10°C (45–50°F). Storage spaces in the home should be cool, dry and dark, such as a cool cupboard, basement or garage, preferably in a north-facing position; store the produce on slatted wooden shelves.

Leaves and herbs

Store leaf varieties, such as salads, spinach and chard, in a plastic bag in the refrigerator. Fresh leaves cannot be stored for long, so it's best to leave them on the plant until you're ready to eat them. Wash salad leaves and put through a salad spinner before storing in a plastic bag. Wash herbs before storing, then treat them as you would a bunch of flowers. Trim off the ends, place them in a glass of water and put them in the refrigerator. You can also cover the tops with a plastic bag to keep the moisture in.

Hard fruits

Apples and pears store very well when wrapped in tissue or newspaper and placed in a wooden box. Wrap each piece of fruit individually. Make sure that the fruits don't touch each other and only store fruits without any damage or bruising. To give them extra protection, add a layer of cardboard between each layer of the fruits.

Well-preserved

Making jams and jellies is an ideal way of storing summer fruits. It's an absolute treat to open up a jar of your luscious homemade jam in the bleak winter months, with memories flooding back of hot, sunny days in the garden as all the flavours of summer hit your taste buds. Fruits and vegetables can also be made into chutneys, relishes or sauces, or bottled using syrup or brine.

Smart storage

Don't wash vegetables or fruits before storing (except salad leaves and herbs); simply brush off soil or dust.

Regularly check stored crops and remove any bad pieces so that they don't infect the others.

Keep fruits and vegetables separate; some fruits can accelerate the ripening of certain vegetables. But if you want to ripen some fruit quickly, put in a paper bag and add an apple or a banana.

Keep tomatoes at room temperature unless they have already been cut, then put them in the refrigerator.

Place kitchen paper under the fruits and vegetables in the refrigerator, which will mop up any moisture. You can also add kitchen paper to a plastic bag containing herbs or salad leaves in the fridge, again to absorb the moisture and make the environment more humid.

OPPOSITE: *Store apples wrapped separately in tissue or newspaper.*

BELOW: *Make jams, preserves and sauces to preserve fruit and vegetables and enjoy your produce over the winter months.*

CHAPTER FOUR

Keeping Animals

This section is an introduction to keeping animals rather than a definitive guide. There are whole books specifically dedicated to animal husbandry with comprehensive information on raising each animal successfully, and you can turn to these more detailed sources once you've decided which you want to keep. Keeping animals entails a huge amount of daily commitment. Therefore, it's essential that you consider very carefully which ones would suit your circumstances as well as your needs.

Once you've decided to venture further in the quest for a greener, more self-sufficient lifestyle, animals are both the most enjoyable and the most satisfying part of having a garden farm. They will frequently put your patience to the test: the naughty goat, given half the chance, will eat through your internet cable, and the adventurous hen will try to consume all your vegetables! However, these same animals will also give you great moments of enjoyment, such as when hens, wings flapping, charge from one end of the garden to compete for the juiciest worm on the end of your fork; or when you catch sight of the goats playing together like puppies; or when you spend ages scratching the bristly back of the pig until it collapses in a state of ecstasy. And what could be better than to start the day with toast spread with honey collected from your own bees.

Before you buy any farm animals, it's important to deal with the legislative side of animal husbandry. Regulations will vary depending on where you live, so contact your local agricultural regulatory body to check whether there are restrictions on keeping animals on your land.

HEN KEEPING
Pets that deliver

Keeping hens is positively the most satisfying aspect of having a garden farm. Once you've made the necessary preparations and taken the plunge to bring home your hens, you'll never look back and you'll be hooked on hen keeping for a very long time. For little cost, hens will provide you with fresh, organic eggs, a lot of fun and a great deal of companionship around the garden.

The nature of chickens

It's rumoured that hen keeping is now the UK's fastest-growing hobby. While nobody really knows how many households keep domestic poultry, with estimates varying wildly between 200,000 and 500,000 households, their popularity is beyond dispute and it's not surprising, since hens have tremendous characters and are busy and productive creatures.

Domesticated chickens can trace their ancestry back to the red jungle fowl of South-East Asia, and retain much of their ancestors' natural behaviour. Given the opportunity, some will still fly and all will scratch, dust bathe and demonstrate not only sensitive and social behaviour but remarkable intelligence as well. Despite their 'chicken brain' reputation, hens have proved that their thinking power is actually quite sophisticated. Perhaps the most fascinating example of this is the chicken's ability to understand that an object, having been taken away and hidden from them, nevertheless continues to exist. This is apparently beyond the capacity of small children.

BELOW: Hens live as a flock and have a sophisticated pecking order.

Getting started

Hens are a 365-days-a-year commitment and rely totally on their owners for their well-being and safety. They'll need a safe, well-structured house and letting out and shutting in every day, and they should be supplied with adequate feed and fresh, clean water. Therefore, consider very carefully before committing to keeping hens who is going to help you out if you have to go away.

Always buy more than one hen. They exist in stable, social groups, recognizing each other by facial features. Studies show that they have 24 distinct cries that communicate an abundance of information to one another, including separate alarm calls depending on whether a predator is travelling by land or water.

Keeping hens in the garden isn't usually a problem, but some areas and gardens may have a poultry restriction order on them, so it's always best to check with your local authority before considering buying them. For instance, there may be a covenant in the property deeds prohibiting the keeping of livestock, including chickens. In any case, your local authority will have grounds for complaint if you keep a noisy cockerel in an urban area or if you fail to keep the chicken feed in an appropriate manner and that results in attracting rats.

Why keep hens?

Soil improvement Hens' droppings will fertilize your soil and activate and enrich your compost heap.

Garden tidying Hens will eat weeds, leftover vegetable crops and windfall fruits.

Pest control Hens are excellent controllers of garden pests and will happily keep down the populations of slugs and snails in the garden.

Waste recycling Hens are great household waste recyclers. You can use old newspapers to line the floor of their house and shredded paper for bedding, and they can feed on garden waste and kitchen scraps.

Food production More than any other pet, hens are productive. They provide you with the delight of collecting eggs from their nest and then cooking and eating a fresh egg every day, which is good for the body and soul.

Health enhancement Hens are great for your health. Even in the depths of winter, you'll be forced to go outside in the fresh air to check on the hens and collect the eggs every day.

Companionship Most of all, hens are wonderful companions and become much-loved members of the family. When you've built up trust with your hens, they will willingly chat and cluck at you, and many hens are quite happy to sit and perch on your arm. My hens are so keen to be part of the family that one day I found my ex-battery hen perching on the back of my sofa in the lounge!

Housing hens

Before you bring your hens home, it's vital to prepare for them. There is an array of hen houses (coops) on the market to choose from, or you may want to convert an old shed or dog kennel and create your own. Whichever you choose, there are some important issues to consider.

Natural habitat Chickens' naturally favour wooded environments with plenty of scrub to scratch around in and where they feel safe. Birds that live in wide open spaces tend never to stray far from their house and the sanctuary it offers from predators. The ideal habitat is free-range with woodland or fruit orchards. Unfortunately, few of us are able to offer this sort of luxurious setting. Those living in urban environments are limited by small plot sizes and minimal overhead vegetation, so a lot of thought and planning is required in order to provide suitable conditions for hens.

Most breeds of chicken prefer to wander where they like, scratching and pecking at plants and insects. Restricting them within a fenced-off area may, therefore, be necessary to avoid ruining precious formal or family gardens where they can cause havoc in vegetable gardens or on lawns.

BELOW: Chickens love to scratch around and forage for tasty morsels to eat.

Choosing a hen house Hen houses can be made of wood or plastic. Timber houses are more natural; they breathe with the seasons and provide a healthy atmosphere. Plastic houses are functional and more modern/urban in design, but they usually offer less space, so make sure that they are suitable for the size hens you intend to buy. With regular cleaning and disinfecting (see opposite), either will provide an appropriate home for your hens.

Hens generally only go into their house at night or during the day to lay an egg. Make sure that the coop is big enough for the quantity of hens you intend to buy. There is often a recommended number of hens per house, depending on the breed. Check with the retailer how many hens a coop is recommended to house, then bear in mind the breed that you intend to keep (see pages 154–156). As a general rule, allow no less than 0.09 sq m (1 sq ft) of floor area per bird in the house and 0.9 sq m (10 sq ft) of space outside; the more space you can give them, the better.

Hen houses should be substantial enough to withstand all weathers. Choose one raised off the ground to prevent it getting damp and rodents nesting beneath. There should be ventilation to prevent respiratory diseases, but it shouldn't be draughty, as hens feel the cold in winter.

Perches Hens need to roost on a perch at night, and the resting position for a hen's foot is a clasping one. The perch should be about 2.5–3 cm (1–1¼ in) wide with rounded edges; a sturdy broom handle makes a good perch. Allow at least 18–20 cm (7–8 in) of perch space per bird and avoid positioning perches too high, as the chickens can injure themselves jumping off. However, as they tend to do half their droppings at night, the perch needs to be high enough to keep a distance from the droppings; it's useful to place a tray below so that the droppings can be cleared away easily.

Nesting areas You generally need one nesting box per four hens. The nesting box is often mounted at the side of the main house, with an outside flap to make collection of the eggs easy. Straw, dust-free shavings or shredded paper are good for lining the nesting box; never use hay, as this can develop a mould that could cause health problems for your hens. Nesting boxes don't have to be large – about 46 cm (18 in) square is usually adequate. Hens will lay anywhere that is nest-like, such as in old fruit crates or a saucepan. They generally like the box to be in a dark, private position, as they tend to go into a trance while laying an egg and don't like to be disturbed.

Hens are fickle, and if you're not finding any eggs in the nesting boxes, try looking around the garden under a bush or on top of a straw bale. One day, I found 30 eggs under an old grape vine; once one hen finds that another hen has laid somewhere else, they all tend to follow suit.

Cleaning the hen house Not the most pleasant of chores, but if you choose or design the house well, the task will be far easier. Cleaning once a week is ideal, but if you use a thick layer of shavings, about 15 cm (6 in) deep, and regularly pick out the droppings (wearing rubber gloves), once a month should be adequate. Straw can also be used as bedding, but tends to become damp more quickly and needs more regular cleaning out. The house should be given a thorough clean every month with a suitable disinfectant, treated with red mite preventative spray and some louse powder sprinkled into the bedding.

Protecting hens It's your responsibility to do your utmost to protect your hens from predators. Foxes are the hens' worst problem, but they also need protection from other predators common in your area, such as badgers, mink, birds of prey and dogs. The hen house should have a hatch that you can close at night to ensure the hens' safety. This can be left open all day so that the hens can go in and out of the house to lay eggs as they please. Hens will be very happy to roam the garden, but

are open to predators if you're not there to protect them. A secure run can provide the solution. This can either be a wired run attached to the house, a fenced run area with the house situated inside or an electric poultry fence. If you're installing a non-electric fence, it needs to be dug in at the base and 1.8 m (6 ft) high.

Hens don't like rain and need to be protected from the sun, so include a shady area within their run where they can take shelter from the weather, including any fierce winds. When weather conditions are extreme, it's a good idea to keep them in the house supplied with food and water.

BELOW: Hens need a ladder with treads leading to their hen house and a pop hole large enough to get through.

Pure breeds – the beauty queens

A pure breed means that the offspring will look exactly like their parents. These birds are often bred for their handsome appearance and beautiful plumage. Some pure breeds tend to go 'off lay' during the winter months. Their lifespan is 3–15 years, but they will go 'off lay' after around 5–6 years. This makes them much more of a pet than a reliable egg layer. There are hundreds of pure breeds, but the following are the most common.

Orpington A large breed with a thick mass of fluffy feathers, named after the town of Orpington in Kent. They were originally bred for the Victorians who wanted a multi-purpose bird that was good for the table and a good layer. They come in an array of colours, the most popular being buff, which is a ginger/gold colour. They also come in black, white, lavender and blue/grey. They are very docile and make excellent family pets. They also make excellent mothers and frequently go broody. Favouring dry conditions, they have a tendency to overeat and become too fat and lazy. They lay about 160 eggs per year.

Light Sussex A very pretty breed with white feathers and speckled black plumage in the neck and tail. Because of their pale plumage they tend to get a little dirty in wet conditions. The eggs are a cream or pale colour. They're a popular choice for the hen keeper, as they're docile and lay about 260 eggs per year.

Speckled Sussex Another hen in the Sussex family, striking in appearance with a typical 'little speckled hen' appeal. They have dark brown feathers speckled with white and an iridescent green shine to their plumage. The speckling on

which breed?

It's vital to consider which breed to buy. Most garden hen keepers prefer a combination of pure breeds, for their stunning looks, and hybrids, for their all-year-round egg-laying capabilities. Pure breeds are relatively expensive, but the cost will vary depending on the breeder, the rarity of the bird and your locality. When deciding on which

Brahma

Buff Orpington

Ex-battery hen

Speckled Sussex

the feathers develops further with age. They are great characters, with a friendly and curious nature. They lay light brown or tinted eggs, about 200 per year.

Brahma This is a stunning breed with amazing feathers and feathered feet that have a tendency to get muddy and clogged up if kept in wet areas. The breed name was shortened from Brahmaputra to Brahma in 1852, when a small flock was given to Queen Victoria. Their origin is not entirely certain, but they are believed to have come from India. They were introduced to the USA in 1846 and to the UK in 1853. They are the ideal breed for the novice hen keeper, being very docile and friendly. These hens also make excellent family pets and are very easy to handle. They lay about 180 eggs per year and have a tendency to go broody.

Rhode Island Red This chicken has dark brown feathers and a dark brown egg. It's a hardy breed, originating from Little Compton in the state of Rhode Island in the USA. They make good pets, but prefer plenty of space to roam. They lay about 260 eggs per year.

Welsummer A beautifully shaped breed with gold and brown feathers, originating from Welsum in Holland. They can have a tendency to be a little flighty, but generally possess a sweet, gentle disposition. I have a Welsummer who frequently flies over the run to get at my prized vegetable patch. They lay a beautiful dark brown egg that is sometimes speckled. They lay about 200 eggs during the course of the year.

breed to buy, it's important to take into account its egg-laying potential. If you come home with half a dozen hybrids that are likely to lay around one egg per day, you could end up with more eggs than you need and you'd have to think very carefully about what to do with the excess eggs.

Mixed Orpington cockerel

Hybrid White Sussex

Orpington cockerel

Light Sussex cockerel

Hybrids – champion egg layers

There are a whole bunch of hybrid breeds – chickens that have been bred specifically for their egg-laying abilities and that usually lay all year round. They are medium-sized and come in a variety of shapes and colours. The brown hybrids are reportedly derived from the Rhode Island Red, and there are also hybrids that resemble Light Sussex as well as a popular speckled hen originating from the Maran, a French breed.

Hybrids generally produce 250–300 eggs per year, have passive natures and are friendly and easy to handle. Their lifespan is about two to four years.

Cross breeds – a bit of both

These are chickens that have been bred from a pure-breed mother and a different pure-breed father. They are often not such good layers as the hybrids, depending on how well they have been bred. Their lifespan is two to ten years.

Bantams – cute and compact

These are small varieties of poultry, generally with lots of personality. They're easier to keep in urban gardens and lay smaller eggs than standard hens.

BELOW: *When picking up a hen, hold it securely above the wings so it can't flap around and cause itself any damage.*

How to handle a hen

You'll need to handle your hens periodically for a variety of reasons. You may simply like to pick them up and pet them, or you may need to give them a louse dust or check for any problems. It's therefore very important that you build up trust with your flock. Call them over when you're scattering corn and get them used to you being around them so that they regard you as a source of comfort and food.

Catching It's best to do this in an unflustered way, and a hen is always easier to catch when it's in its housing area and it's getting dark, which means it too is calm as well as contained. Tempt the hen to come to you by using some corn or a treat. If you need to catch it during the day, try coaxing it with some food and then bring both your hands down over the back, holding the wings against the body so that it can't flap.

Holding Once you've managed to catch the hen and it feels calm and secure, hold it closely against your body using one hand to support it underneath so that it feels secure against you.

BELOW: *Pick up and handle your hen often to gain its trust; it will soon enjoy the contact with you and be relaxed.*

Classic chicken behaviour

Pecking order Hens have a natural pecking order, and you'll soon see who eats first, who charges across the garden to get at the treats ahead of the others and who gets pushed to the back of the queue when lining up to go into the hen house.

When introducing new hens into the group, it's best done at night. Wait until the hens have put themselves to bed and they're all quiet, then gently put the new hen or hens into the sleeping area. That way they will all come out together in the morning after spending a peaceful night together. If possible, it's best to introduce two hens at a time, rather than singly, so that a new arrival will have some company while the others are getting used to them.

Dust baths Chickens love to dust bathe, rolling around in dry, soft soil and throwing dust through their feathers with their wings. This is a natural way for hens to clean themselves and helps keep their feathers free of lice. If you're keeping the hens enclosed in a run, be sure to provide them with a dry area where they can take their dust baths. A deep tray filled with light, fine soil or compost will be more than adequate; it must be fine enough to fill the breathing pores of the lice to kill them.

Scratching Given the choice, chickens usually much prefer to range freely, foraging for food by using their claws to scratch the soil and pecking vigorously at the ground. They move constantly, turning over and raking the earth looking for seeds, insects for valuable protein and small stones or grit that they ingest to grind up the food in their gizzard – a process akin to humans using their teeth. If given half the chance they will scratch up any young shoots. Scratching will help keep their claws down and naturally keep them busy all day.

BELOW: Hens love to relax and dust bathe.

Feeding and drinking

A chicken will eat 125–130 g (about 4½ oz) per day including plants, insects, worms and slugs. But before you get too excited at the thought of them consuming all the slugs in your vegetable patch, think again because they'll also devour the young vegetables and scratch up young shoots.

Studies have shown that at least a quarter of a chicken's diet can be flies and a further half weeds and other plant wastes, and their egg laying will still be equal to that of chickens raised entirely on commercial feed. Hens still have the instinct not to eat poisonous plants, but there's always one...

It's a good idea to provide hens with a suitable area where they can forage and also a feeder topped up with a complete food to ensure that they get the nutrients they need all year round. You can add flax seed to their food, which boosts the omega-3 fatty acid content of their eggs.

Water On average, a hen will drink 250 ml (9 fl oz) of water per day. Make sure that your hens have access to fresh, clean water at all times. If possible, hang the drink container or stand on some bricks to prevent dust and soil from being kicked up into it. There are poultry tonics available that you can add to their drinking water. They contain a blend of herbal oils that give the hens an

What to feed

Layers' pellets This is a complete food compressed into pellet form. If the hens are laying, these pellets should be available for them to peck at as they choose. Traditional layers' pellets can sometimes be too large for bantams, but smaller bantam pellets are available.

Layers' mash This is the same food as contained in layers' pellets, but ground into a coarse, grainy powder. It takes the hens longer to eat, keeping them occupied for longer, particularly if they're enclosed in a pen, but they will also pick out only the pieces they like, whereas the elements are evenly mixed in the pellets.

Mixed corn This is a high-energy food; feeding too much can make your hens fat. Use this as a treat, a little like a dessert. As a guide, feed one handful per hen and scatter it on the ground so that they have to work for it. Corn is a very good incentive for the hens to come to call if you want them to go into their run or coop, or move them away from the vegetable garden. Mixed corn is the ingredient that makes the yolks in the eggs bright yellow.

Kitchen scraps Hens love these, and you'll soon discover their favourites – usually pasta, rice, cheese and a small amount bread, particularly if it's soaked in milk. It's best to boil up any root vegetables, as they don't like them raw. Make sure that the scraps you feed are fresh and contain no meat or excess salt. Don't overfeed your hens on scraps or they will not be getting a balanced diet.

Grit When hens take in food, it's held in the digestive system and then passes into the gizzard, which has strong muscular walls that contract to grind up the food. It's essential that hens take in small pieces of grit or stones that sit in the gizzard to help break up the food. Mixed grit is a combination of grit and crushed oyster shell that also gives hens some added calcium and keeps their eggshells from going soft.

extra boost during the moulting season, if they have any environmental change or if they're generally low in condition and need a pick-me-up.

Feeders and drinkers There is a variety of feeders available, some plastic and others galvanized, the latter longer lasting. Some of them have a sheltered top to keep the food dry if it's kept in an exposed area. With all types of feeder, it's essential to put the feed away at night to prevent unwelcome rodents. Clear away droppings from the feeding and drinking area to avoid contamination of any food or water.

Tip: The wild bird population will also be very keen on consuming your chickens' food. To deter them, try suspending old CDs around the feeder.

BELOW. Hens will often gather together around the feeding and drinking area – a little like co-workers gathering around the water cooler in the office.

What not to feed

Raw green potato peelings These contain a toxic substance called solanine.

Anything very salty Can cause salt poisoning.

Citrus fruit and peel

Dried or raw/undercooked beans These contain a toxic substance called haemaglutin.

Avocado skin and stone These contain low levels of toxicity.

Raw eggs You don't want to introduce your chickens to the tastiness of eggs, otherwise they will be tempted to eat the uncollected eggs in the nesting boxes.

Sweets, chocolate and sugar These are bad for a chicken's digestive system; chocolate can be poisonous to most pets.

Hen health

If your hens have plenty of space and you regularly clean and maintain their coop, they shouldn't suffer any health problems. However, it's worth making regular checks just in case something crops up. Read the list below so that you learn how to identify and deal with common problems.

Routine health check Good health results in firm droppings, a bright red comb and bright, beady eyes. Hens should appear alert and busy, and be plump but not too fat.

If a hen is sick, it generally looks huddled up with its tail pointed downwards. The comb can often look pale or flopped over and it can be off its feed and off lay.

Common health problems: how to spot and treat

Problem	Recommended treatment
Worms	Chickens should be wormed regularly. Use a natural, herb-based wormer to avoid any 'off lay' period, which can come in a pellet form that you sprinkle in their feed or in a liquid form that you put into their drinking water. If the hens are free-range, the liquid form is often more reliable, as they don't always eat all their pellets every day, but they have to drink. Follow the instructions on the packet or bottle.
Red mites	These little dust-sized grey/brown mites are probably a hen's worst nightmare, becoming red by sucking its blood. They only live on a hen for a couple of hours, usually at night. Once they have had their feast, they will move into the crevices and gaps in the house. If you have red mites in your hen house, the hens will look anaemic and will stop laying. During the day, check under the perches for mites. The best method of avoiding them is prevention. Red mite solutions are available that you can dilute and use to spray the whole hen house once a month. Alternatively, use a red mite powder, paying particular attention to dusting perches, corners and gaps. Also regularly use a red mite dust directly onto the hen for prevention and treatment.
Lice	These will live on the floor of the hen house and on the chickens themselves. They will also find their way into the hens' dust baths. Check monthly under the wings, around the vent and through the feathers. Lice will cause feather loss and extreme discomfort. Dust your hens regularly with louse powder to avoid this.
Wounds	Clean any wound or cut with clean warm water and spray with a veterinary antibacterial aerosol. If the cut has healed over but looks as though there is pus underneath, try mixing together some petroleum jelly and runny honey and spreading it gently onto the affected area. This has the effect of drawing the pus out of the wound.
Limping	Check for any broken legs and underneath the feet in case the hen has caught its foot on anything sharp. The hen could also have an ailment called bumble foot, where the underside of the foot contains pus that will need draining and treating. Broken legs are a problem and the bird may need to be culled or put down by the vet.

Coping with a sick hen The first thing to do is to separate the ailing hen from the other hens to protect it from being bullied or pecked. Putting it in a completely separate area is ideal, but if you don't have the space available to do this, use a large box tipped on its side. Put plenty of wood shavings or straw inside to keep it warm and make sure that food and water are available. Quite often a hen will make a full recovery within hours, but if it doesn't seem to be improving, do seek advice from a vet who has knowledge of chickens.

Problem	Recommended treatment
Blocked crop	Food can get stuck in the crop, the area where it's stored before it reaches the gizzard for digestion. New hens unused to free-ranging are prone to this problem, as they eat too quickly and the food gets blocked. Use a teaspoon or a syringe (without the needle) to pour a little olive oil into the mouth, then massage the neck gently to try to release the blockage. Natural live yoghurt is also very effective. Sometimes holding the hen upside down and massaging the neck is also useful in releasing the blockage. Do this very gently and try to keep the beak open while massaging the contents down towards the beak.
Egg bound	This can sometimes be caused by an unbalanced diet and too many scraps. The hen will look miserable and keep going in and out of the nest box to try to lay the egg, which is stuck in the oviduct. This is a very serious condition and a swift response is necessary, as the hen can quickly die. Place petroleum jelly around the rim of the vent. Hold the hen high above a saucepan of boiling water so that the steam bathes the vent area and relaxes it, taking care not to scald the hen. If the egg breaks inside, the hen risks critical infection.
Scaly leg mites	A chicken's leg is covered in scales, and should be smooth and clean. Scaly leg mites live underneath the scales and cause the scales to lift off. Treat this by bathing the legs in surgical spirit twice a week until the mites have disappeared.
Moulting	Hens will moult once or twice a year. This can be quite disconcerting, especially when they lose most of their feathers. When I first started keeping hens, I thought something terrible was happening to them, as some of them became almost bald. This is perfectly normal and the feathers will grow back. They will also go 'off lay' while they are going through the moult.
Droppings	These should be firm with a white cap. Sometimes the droppings will become runny, which is nothing to be alarmed about, as by nature hens eat a huge variety of foods. But if the problem persists, consult a vet.
Blocked vent	Some heavily feathered breeds will often have dirty feathers around their vent, in which case check regularly and clean as necessary so that it doesn't become blocked.

Daily hen care routine

Morning Your hens will have had a very peaceful night, perching with their eyes closed. Like other birds, as soon as it's dawn they will wake up and want to come out of their house to feed and drink. Chickens won't come out before it's light – they can't see well in the dark and will be nervous of predators. Once you've opened up the coop and the hens come out of their house, this is a good chance to check each one over to see if they're all well. Ensure that they have enough food and drink for the day. If the hens are confined to a run, make sure that you put some greens in their run for them to peck or make a new area of grass available to them.

At some point during the morning, they'll go into their nesting area to lay an egg. The rest of the day, they will go about scratching, eating and having a dust bath. On a hot sunny day, they may sunbathe, when they lie down and stretch one wing out to absorb the rays of the sun.

Check for any eggs that have been laid and remove them from the nests.

Evening Hens will naturally start to make their way back to their house as it starts to get dark. Usually before darkness falls they'll put themselves into their house and perch ready for the night. Then all you have to do is close their hatch securely.

Hens are at their most vulnerable at dusk or at night when foxes and other common predators are most prevalent.

LEFT: *A happy, healthy hen will have an alert, beady eye and a bright comb and wattle.*

OPPOSITE: *Hens love to feast on kitchen scraps: pasta is always a favourite.*

Seasonal hen care routine

Regular cleaning out of the hens' housing is vital to their welfare. Remove any droppings in order to keep the nesting areas and hen house clean. Make monthly checks for red mite and lice (see page 160).

Spring and summer This is the hens' favourite time of year when there is an abundance of bugs, grubs and warmer weather. The longer daylight hours will mean that they will lay more eggs than in the colder months. Make sure that you give them extra water in the summer, as they'll quickly become thirsty on long, hot days. The hens could go broody during the spring or summer, so collect their eggs regularly to help prevent this. When the sun gets very hot, the hens will take refuge in the shade. If your garden hasn't any natural shade from trees or bushes, make sure that you provide a shady area for them.

If your hens are free-range, they may go further afield in the spring and summer months, so check they that all come back at night.

Hens generally moult in the late summer, which is a natural process. Egg laying may stop at this time, and if so, check that they're eating a balanced diet.

Autumn and winter Chickens are very hardy and are protected from the cold by their thick feathers, but they hate getting wet. They will run for cover if the weather is rainy or windy, or stay in their house. Make sure that you provide them with an area where they can shelter from the elements. In freezing conditions, check their water twice a day in case it freezes over.

Some hens go 'off lay' in the autumn or winter. Keep an eye on them to check that they've not stopped laying eggs for any other reasons.

When it's really frosty, the hens can get frostbite on their combs and wattles. Rubbing a little petroleum jelly onto large wattles or combs can help prevent this problem. Severe frostbite requires veterinary attention.

Rats and mice can be a problem at this time of year. Put the feed out of reach at night to discourage vermin.

Check the chickens' housing and make sure that its waterproof, as they need to keep warm and dry at night.

Egg know-how Eggs from your own hens are an excellent, satisfying source of energy. They taste delicious and are a real bonus to hen keeping. They come in all different colours and sizes, depending on the breed of hen you are keeping (see pages 154–156).

When a point-of-lay (young) hen starts laying, the eggs can be quite small, but the bigger the hen gets, the larger the egg becomes. Sometimes you'll find an unusual-shaped egg. This is quite normal; shop-bought eggs are uniform in size and shape because the misshapen ones are discarded.

Eggs don't need to be stored in the refrigerator; keep them pointed-end down in a cool place and they will last for up to three weeks.

Soft shells can be caused by a lack of calcium in the hens' feed. Ensure that your hens are given plenty of oyster shell or mixed grit. Another solution is to feed them broken eggshells mixed into their pellets or mash.

During the spring/summer months the hens should be laying at their optimum. Sometimes this means that you'll have more eggs than you can eat. Think carefully about what to do with your eggs. They are often a welcome gift for family and friends who appreciate eating fresh eggs without keeping hens.

Tip: A good test to see if an egg is fresh is by putting it in a bowl of water. If it floats, it's rotten; if it sinks, it's fresh.

LEFT: A great pleasure of keeping hens is to collect fresh eggs every day.

OPPOSITE: A broody hen will spread herself out flat and be very moody if disturbed from the nest.

Raising chicks

After you've kept hens for a while, you may want to raise your own chicks. This is a very exciting and interesting process. There is something very appealing about watching a mother hen and her little brood running around your garden farm, or a bunch of little incubator-raised chicks running over to you because they think you're their mum.

There are two methods of raising chicks
Option 1: The broody hen In the spring, some hens will go broody. This is by far the easiest way to raise babies, as the broody hen will do most, if not all, of the job for you.

If you have a cockerel, this will usually mean that the eggs will be fertilized. If you don't have a cockerel, you can buy fertilized (hatching) eggs. Simply remove the non-fertilized eggs from under the broody hen and replace them with the fertilized eggs. It's best to do this when the hen is away eating or drinking, or at night.

Don't be too quick to put the hatching eggs under a broody hen – leave her for a few days to make sure that she is well and truly broody. A hen that isn't truly broody may leave the nest, having decided not to be broody any more, and the fertilized eggs will be ruined.

A normal clutch of eggs is 9–15, but a hen will be happy to sit on less and it depends on the breed of hen as to how many she can sit on comfortably. The hybrid breeds that are bred for egg laying are less likely to go broody. Good broody breeds are Orpingtons, Brahmas, Sussexes and Silkies.

A broody hen will make herself very large and flat by fluffing out her feathers, and if you remove her from the nest, she will cluck around and be very agitated. She will usually stop laying eggs after a few days from being broody and will stay on her nest all day, only leaving for a short time to feed, drink and to take a dust bath. Place her food and drink away from her to force her to leave the nest. You can then check the nest and remove any droppings so that she doesn't soil her eggs. The hen will sit on the eggs and incubate them at the correct temperature for 21 days.

How to spot a broody hen

Stays in her nest and doesn't want to move.

Pecks some of the feathers on her chest; this is so that she has more body contact with the eggs to keep them at the right temperature.

Clucking and agitated noises when approached.

Less sociable and in a kind of trance.

Option 2: Using an incubator If you don't have a broody hen or if your hen is reluctant to sit on the eggs for long enough, you can use an incubator – a very effective, artificial way of hatching chicks. There are several incubators on the market that perform the whole role of a broody hen, keeping the eggs at exactly the right temperature and turning them automatically every couple of hours. Choose unsoiled eggs to put into the incubator, but don't wash them, as this removes the natural protective film on the outside of the shell.

The incubator needs to be checked regularly to ensure that the temperature is constant. It's best to keep it in an undisturbed place and always check the manufacturer's instructions, as some incubators will need added water to keep the humidity at the right level.

OPPOSITE: *A chick born in an incubator will soon be tame and think you're its mother.*

BELOW: *Chicks will be taken out very soon after hatching by their mother and taught the skills of foraging.*

Hatching

Whether using an incubator or a broody hen, at around 19–20 days you will hear some cheeping from the eggs. Leave the eggs alone and don't be tempted to lift them to inspect them, as this will disturb the broody hen and can turn them the wrong way for hatching.

Chicks have a little sharp part on their beaks specially designed for cutting through the shell. It's quite normal for some eggs not to hatch. They will either be unfertilized or some eggs will contain dead chicks. These need to be removed from the nest or the incubator. If they have still not hatched around 22–23 days, they're unlikely to hatch.

What happens with the broody hen The hen should have been separated from the rest of the flock and have her own private space where she is undisturbed by the other birds. She will do all the hatching for you. When the chicks start to hatch, she will sit on the eggs until they have all hatched. Chicks can live for up to 72 hours by feeding on the internal yolk sac from the egg, which provides all their nutritional needs.

What to do next Once the chicks have all hatched, the hen will bring them out to feed and drink. Her behaviour will change and she will start clucking and acting like a fussy mother. The chicks will need fresh water and chick crumb (see page 168). The hen makes a particular clucking sound, which teaches the chicks that it's time to eat, and they will copy the hen and very soon start eating and drinking. It's important to provide a suitable chick drinker, as chicks can easily drown if they get stuck in a water bowl.

There is no need to buy a special feed for the mother hen at this point, as she will be fed perfectly well on the same feed.

If you have an enclosed, protected area of grass, the hen will be very happy to potter around showing the chicks what they can and can't eat. Protect the hen and the chicks from the rest of the flock as well as predators, as a jealous flock member may try to give the chicks a dangerous peck if they think the chicks are getting more food than them.

When the chicks get tired or cold, they will nest underneath the feathers of the hen, and she will call them to her if she feels that they are unsafe or getting cold. The mother will automatically become very protective and this is often enough to ward off the other hens and to protect them from predators. It's best to keep the mother and chicks in their separate space at night until the chicks are nearly adult and big enough to defend themselves.

What happens with the incubator The eggs will hatch after around 21 days. When the chicks emerge they will be wet and sticky, so leave them in the incubator until they are dry and fluffy before removing them to a heated area.

What to do next Incubated chicks require heat to survive, provided by a heat lamp suspended above their container. The temperature that they need during the first week is around 35°C (95°F). From then on the heat can be dropped 2°C (5°F) each week by gradually raising the heat lamp.

It's often difficult to get the temperature right for the chicks. A rule of thumb is if they are all huddled in the centre of the heat source and cheeping a lot, they are too cold. If they are all spread out to the outside edges of the heat, they are too hot. They should be equally spread around the heat.

They will need a heat source up to around six weeks. After that, gently take the heat away by raising the heat lamp over a few days so that they get used to the lower temperature. Only part of their area should be heated, as the chicks need to be able to cool off when they need to. If the chicks become too cold, they will all huddle together and can sometimes get smothered, so it's important for the chicks to have fresh air to prevent them from overheating.

The chicks will need a constant supply of fresh water and chick crumb (see page 168). You can act as 'mum' by gently dipping their beaks in the food and water; once one of them starts to eat and drink, the others will shortly follow suit.

Hatching rescue There are some people that don't like to interfere with the hatching process, as they say that the chicks that don't hatch are likely to be handicapped and things are best left to nature. I have hatched several broods using both an incubator and a broody hen. I tend to leave broody hens to their own devices, but if a chick has been cheeping for over 12 hours and the egg has cracked and the chick hasn't emerged, I have peeled away the shell to help the chick along. You have to be very gentle, as the egg can sometimes stick to the side of the chick, so it's best to take your time, perhaps in spite of an anxious, noisy chick.

This approach is entirely at your discretion and you take your own chances as to whether the chick thrives or not. In my own experience, the assisted incubated chicks have always done well, and the only times I've had a handicapped chick is with a broody hen.

Feeding and watering A chick starter feed (chick crumb) should be fed to all chicks until they are six weeks of age, and they will always need fresh, clean water. At around 20–25 weeks, feed them a pullet grower feed, after which they can be switched to layers' pellets or mash (see page 158).

Cockerel or hen? When raising chicks, it is very hard to be able to tell if they're male or female. Some breeds have been bred so that the sexes can be differentiated according to their colour as chicks, either paler or darker, in order that the males can be culled immediately at birth. Most breeds are very difficult to sex and it may not be until they start to crow at 25 weeks that you'll know if you have a cockerel or a hen.

Cock-a-doodle-doo or don't?

There is no reason to keep a cockerel unless you intend to breed chickens; hens live perfectly well as a group without a cockerel. There are often restrictions on keeping cockerels and they can soon upset your neighbours, depending on where you live. Of course, some people love the sound of a cockerel crowing, but it's best to check this out with your neighbours before you embark on buying one. The recommended ratio of cockerels to hens is one cockerel to ten hens.

LEFT: *A Buff Orpington cockerel may be a magnificent beast, but not at 5 o'clock in the morning when you've had a late night.*

OPPOSITE: *A Brahma can act as the perfect surrogate mum for these baby Buff Orpington chicks which were raised from bought hatching eggs when there wasn't a cockerel.*

BEEKEEPING
Making life sweeter

Keeping bees and collecting honey is one of the most wonderful antidotes to the stresses of 21st-century living. In beekeeping, you have to be slow and gentle, in tune with the weather and understand the natural order of the flowering season, but unlike most hobbies you will be handsomely rewarded with the most delicious result – your own honey from your garden farm, along with total inner contentment.

Getting started

If you are a complete beginner to beekeeping, the best advice is to contact the branch of your local beekeeping organization. Many groups hold novice training sessions; others will set you up with a 'buddy', who will always be on hand to help you through the first few years and also likely to offer you access to second-hand equipment as well as good-tempered bees.

all about hives

All hives are made of boxes, without tops or bottoms, stacked one above the other, with a floor at the very bottom and a roof at the top.

Like a filing cabinet, each box is then hung with a series of frames that contain sheets of wax.

The bees 'draw out' this wax template, known as foundation, to make comb, which is then

used either to raise the young, known as 'brood', or to store the honey.

Bees store the honey in the upper parts of a hive, while the queen lays in the lower part. By inserting an artificial barrier – a mesh usually referred to as a 'queen excluder' – through which the smaller worker bees can pass but the bigger queen cannot, you can guarantee that the lower brood chamber contains the queen, eggs and larvae, and is separated from the upper boxes (known as the 'supers') where all the honey is stored.

Hives are best positioned in a sunny but shaded spot facing into a prevailing wind, as it helps the bees when they return full of nectar. If you live in a garden, face them 1–1.2 m (3–4 ft) away from a high structure, such as a shed, fence or hedge, so that the bees will then emerge from the hive and fly straight up and away. If you have more than one hive, leave around 1 m (3 ft) between each, but most importantly angle the entrances in different directions.

Which hive?

Most beginners start with the easy-to-handle British National, which looks like a stack of square brown boxes. However, the more aesthetic choice is the traditional white WBC hive (the initials are those of the original designer), which although more difficult to grapple with (it has a more complicated construction with a double skin) is worth it for the sake of appearance alone.

RIGHT: A traditional white wooden hive is a beautiful addition to your garden farm.

Beekeeping kit – and bees

In addition to a hive, you will also need two basic tools: a smoker and a hive tool. The smoker is used to puff smoke around the hive as you work, which calms the bees. Keeping this alight is in itself a major skill and everyone will have their favourite fuel – old egg boxes work especially well. A hive tool has a hook and a flat end, and is used to prise apart all the different hive parts. Like with any hobby, beyond these two essential items there are hundreds of different gadgets and widgets on offer, and if you take up beekeeping, never again will your relations be stumped for a birthday or Christmas gift for you.

When it comes to clothing, as a beginner opt for maximum protection. An all-in-one suit with veil, together with a good pair of gloves and a stout pair of wellies, will give you the confidence to open up that hive for the first time.

And finally, you'll need some bees! Seek advice from fellow beekeepers, but most importantly do make sure they are gentle. Temperamentally, bees can vary a great deal, and as a beginner you really do need to have quiet bees that will be forgiving of your less than perfect bee-handling skills.

Your local beekeeping association may also be able to provide you with bees, or you can buy a nucleus – a colony of honeybees that is smaller than a fully established colony – from specialist companies. Visit a bee auction (see below) or alternatively ask a beekeeping friend to look out for a swarm in late spring.

The start-up bill So how much will all this cost? If you were to buy everything new, you could expect to pay at least £300 for a complete hive with bees and tools, and £100 for clothing. However, look out for your local beekeeping association's bee auction, which usually takes place in late spring, where you can expect to pick up many of the items secondhand for a fraction of the price of new.

LEFT: Use the smoker to calm the bees while you check the hive.

BELOW: A hive tool is handy for hooking frames out of the hive.

RIGHT: Adequate protection is vital to give you confidence around the hive.

The private life of the honeybee

Unlike most other insects, honeybees don't hibernate during the winter. Instead, they survive by having a large workforce of up to 50,000 bees in the summer to collect nectar and make honey, and by then reducing their number to only 10,000 bees in the winter, which live off the honey to keep warm.

Each individual bee is a selfless member of a highly developed society known as a colony. Worker bees make up 99 per cent of the bees in a colony and are all female. Their life expectancy depends on their workload, with a busy summer bee wearing herself out in six weeks, while a far less active autumn-hatched bee will survive six months through the winter.

During the busy summer months, the job description of individual hive inhabitants will depend on their age: 0–4 days after hatching they are employed cleaning and feeding larvae, at 6–14 days they start a few test flights but are mainly involved with housework and guard duties and at 14–21 days they are wax producers, making and repairing combs. Only after three weeks do they commence foraging for nectar, which they bring back to the hive. The housebound bees then work hard to reduce the water content of the nectar and so turn it into honey.

Each colony contains one queen. She is half as large again as a worker bee and can live up to three years, during which time she could produce over half a million eggs. A queen is produced when the worker bees decide to feed a larva royal jelly. Shortly after hatching she makes a maiden flight, mates with six or seven males (drones) and then returns to the hive never to leave again, unless the colony swarms. On a day-to-day basis, all the queen's needs are met by the worker bees, but in addition to producing eggs, she also releases a pheromone scent that allows worker bees to identify their own hive and recognize foreign invaders.

The only purpose of the drones is reproduction and they are tolerated on an altruistic basis during the spring and summer when they wander hobo-like from hive to hive. Each morning, as long as the weather is fine, the drones leave the colony and fly around at about 20 m (65 ft), waiting for a virgin queen. Should one happen along, they will enthusiastically mate on the wing, although this is a selfless act, as in doing so the drone's genitals literally explode inside the queen and the male bee falls to the ground and dies.

The mated queen then returns to the hive where she commences laying eggs, peaking at about 1,500 eggs a day, for up to three years.

BELOW: *In the summer there may be up to 50,000 bees in the colony.*

BELOW: *This frame contains part of the brood nest.*

A year in the life of a beekeeper

It's all well and good making a month-by-month list of the tasks that you'll need to complete, but with climate change wreaking havoc on seasonal weather patterns, this is no longer a reliable indicator, and the best way to judge what needs to be done in the apiary is to look at which plants are in flower and act accordingly. Here's a quick rundown of the basic tasks.

Spring

Once the first crocuses are out in early spring, visit your hive on a sunny day to make sure that the bees are out and about. This is a good time to check that they still have some honey left – lift the hive, and if it's very light, feed the bees with a solution of sugar and water. Don't open the hive.

As soon as you can be outside without a jumper on, it's time to open up the hive for a thorough examination and spring clean. You need to find your queen, check that she is laying eggs and make sure there are still enough honey stores.

Once the hawthorn blossom is out in about mid- to late spring, beware – you are entering the swarming season and you need to check the hive every ten days. You are looking to ensure that the queen is laying a healthy brood and checking for queen cells, which is a sign that they are going to swarm and you'll need to do something about it.

To reduce the likelihood of swarming, make sure there is plenty of egg-laying space in the brood chamber and plenty of room for storing honey in the supers above, adding another if necessary.

Summer

When the lime trees are in flower in late spring/early summer, your bees will be enjoying the peak honey flow. Keep a regular check on how quickly they are filling the supers, and once the top super is 70 per cent occupied by stores and/or bees, add another super.

Unless you live near heather moors, once the rosebay willowherb finishes flowering, the honey flow will more or less have finished, usually in midsummer. At this point, collect your honey!

First, you need to clear the bees from the honey using a clever one-way traffic device known as a 'porter bee escape', a single-way valve inserted into a wooden board and placed between the brood and the frames of honey that you want to collect. When

the bees leave the honey frames, they can't get back, so the frames can be collected free of bees. Insert the porter bee escape in the morning, and the following evening when it's dusk and the bees aren't flying, go back to the hive to collect the bee-free supers full of frames of honey.

Each super can weigh 13 kg (30 lb), 1.3 kg (3 lb) a frame, so you will need a wheelbarrow, and don't forget to leave at least one super full of honey for the bees.

Once back home you will need to have the use of a spinner – most beekeeping associations have these to loan out to members. To spin the honey from the frames, uncap the frame of honey and put it into the spinner, which works by centrifugal force, or you

can buy electric ones. Give the empty frames (known as wet frames) back to the bees to clean out before removing them for winter storage. The honey collects at the base of the spinner, which has a tap. Fill sterilized jars and seal with a lid. The honey will last literally hundreds of years!

In a good summer you should expect to harvest at least 18 kg (40 lb) of honey per hive, and many experienced beekeepers will do much better than that.

Finally, you need to replace the 'stolen' honey by feeding your bees with a cane sugar solution, 450 g (1 lb) of white granulated cane sugar to 568 ml (1 pint) of water, remembering that each hive needs 16 kg (35 lb) of honey stored to safely see the bees through the winter. The solution is put into a feeder (another piece of kit) and inverted over the frames for the bees to digest and turn into honey.

Beeswax can be collected on a small scale by removing the wax during the honey extraction process. Melt in an old saucepan.

Autumn

In mid-autumn give the bees a last check before winter and in particular guard against unwelcome winter visitors. Place metal mouse guards across the hive entrance, pin some plastic sacks around the outside to deter woodpeckers and then place a couple of heavy bricks on the roof of the hive to keep everything secure in the event of rough, stormy weather.

Winter

Leave your bees well alone and DON'T ever open the hive. When, however, there is a sunny day, take a look at the hive, as you should expect to see a few bees out and about enjoying the sunshine.

Swarming

Being wild creatures, bee colonies survive perfectly happily without any human intervention, building up numbers in the spring, making honey in the summer and then reducing numbers again in the winter to live off the stores. However, bees recognize a colony as a single unit, and in order to reproduce a second colony, they naturally go through a process known as swarming.

This involves the old queen and all the flying bees leaving the hive in search of a new home. A queen cell, which will provide a new queen, and all the hive-bound bees are left behind. So while your original colony will still exist, and indeed grow over the season, that summer's workforce will be seriously depleted, which considerably reduces the amount of honey you will collect during that year.

Swarming is a complex subject. A multitude of books have been written about it and there are many schools of thought on how to deal with the swarming problem, so master the art of swarm control and you really are on the way to becoming a serious beekeeper.

Bee stings

It's inevitable that you will get stung at some point, particularly when you're new to beekeeping. Remove the sting and apply an antihistamine cream or take an antihistamine tablet. Bee stings are not usually a problem unless you're stung on the face or throat, in which case visit a doctor. Some people also have allergies or bad reactions to bee stings; again, seek medical advice or attention if this is the case.

Honey

This rich, golden liquid is loved by cultures all over the world. It's not only delicious simply eaten on toast but can be used to replace sugar in cooking and baking. Nothing is ever added or taken away from honey; it needs no preservatives and is totally natural. Honey is sweeter than sugar, so when using honey in place of sugar in a recipe, only use two-thirds as much as you would sugar.

Honey has a distinctive flavour, aroma and colour, factors determined by the type of flower from which the bee collects the nectar. Honey takes on the characteristics of the herb, tree or flower that the bee has visited, such as lavender, apple blossom, dandelion, rosemary or thyme. Although most hives will select nectar from a variety of flowers, some hives live off a single type of flower and this is very keenly sought by beekeepers.

Honey will crystallize if it is stored at too cold a temperature; it resists crystallization best when kept at about 21°C (70°F). It can also crystallize if moisture gets into the jar from a wet spoon or if left unsealed in a damp environment. To liquefy crystallized honey, stand the jar in a bowl of hot water until the crystals dissolve. When storing, keep honey in an airtight container at room temperature.

In the UK, over 25,000 tonnes (tons) of honey are consumed every year, spread on bread, drizzled over cereals, used in baking and cooking or eaten off the spoon. There are also many different varieties available from all over the world offering a wide range of exotic flavours. In the USA there are more than 300 unique types of honey from various flower sources, such as clover, eucalyptus and orange blossom.

Baby warning It's recommended that babies under 12 months old should not be given honey to eat. This is because their digestive tract hasn't yet developed enough to process some of the naturally occurring constituents in honey, causing potential feeding problems.

Fascinating facts about honey

Did you know that…

Honey can be used to treat sore throats and coughs, cuts and burns. It has been recognized as a natural medicine for thousands of years.

When a bee finds a good source of nectar, it flies back to the hive and shows its friends where the nectar source is by performing a kind of dance, positioning the flower in relation to the sun and the hive. This is known as the 'waggle dance'.

Honey lasts for a very long time: an explorer who found a 2,000-year-old jar of honey in an Egyptian tomb said it still tasted delicious.

ABOVE: *It's vital to make regular checks of the brood nest during the season.*

KEEPING GOATS

There are several reasons for keeping goats – for their milk, meat or fleece, or as pets – and the breed of goat you choose will be determined by the reason you want to keep them. If you intend milking or breeding goats for meat, it's best to consult a specific manual or to make contact with an experienced goat keeper, who will be able to give you details on how to milk and make cheese or how to butcher and produce your own meat. Whatever your reason for keeping goats, you'll find them fascinating, curious creatures and great companions in your garden farm.

Goats are herd animals and therefore you should always keep more than one. Some people keep goats as companions for other animals such as horses, but ideally, goats prefer the company of other goats; even in large herds, goats will often choose a 'best friend' to hang out with.

Gearing up for goats Whatever your reason for keeping goats, make contact with a recommended breeder when you've chosen the breed you want. Contact with your local goat-keeping society will provide you with an invaluable source of information on goat breeds, local breeders and goat keeping. When transporting goats, it's best if you collect them in a closed van or a horsebox or trailer. Sometimes the breeder will deliver them to you.

Most goats (except pygmies – see panel bottom left for a list of breeds) are dehorned at a young age to protect both the goat and people.

Goat-keeping essentials Goats take up little space, are inexpensive to maintain, generally easy to handle and need only simple housing. As long as their shelter is well ventilated, free from draughts and protects them from the elements (goats hate rain), they will be perfectly happy. A simple garden shed can be turned into goat housing. One single goat requires around 19 sq m (200 sq ft) outdoors. A miniature breed needs around 12 sq m (130 sq ft).

Fencing is particularly important when keeping goats. They are renowned escape artists and will

Which breed?

Popular breeds of goat include:
Angora – especially used for their fleece or mohair
Anglo Nubian
Toggenburg
La Mancha
Pygmy – a miniature breed, particularly popular as a pet

jump over or work their way under anywhere that isn't secure. It's recommended to erect a well-posted, wire-mesh fence 1.2–1.5 m (4–5 ft) high around their field, or you can use an electric wire-strand fence. As long as goats are well fed and not too bored, they will generally stay put. Don't, however, position them within eyesight of your valued vegetable plot, otherwise the temptation for them may be too much and you'll be constantly struggling to keep them contained. By nature, goats love climbing, so make sure there are no areas around the fencing for them to springboard from and make a bid for freedom.

Goats will damage your trees and hedges if given half the chance. Anything that they shouldn't eat they will, so it's important to keep them confined to spaces where they can't come into contact with the things they shouldn't eat.

Goats won't keep your grass down like other grazing animals; they prefer scrubland. You'll need to supplement their diet by feeding with specially formulated goat-mix feed and they'll need some extra hay in the winter. They also benefit from a mineral lick, which is particularly useful if they're confined and don't have much access to open spaces. A goat will taste things by using its lips.

Young goats will carry objects around and play with them, much the same as puppies. Watch that they don't play with sharp objects such as tin cans – they're not trying to eat them, just exploring.

OPPOSITE: *Young kids enjoy exploring, escaping and searching through hedgerows.*

RIGHT: *Always keep more than one goat – a lone goat is not a happy one.*

KEEPING PIGS

Pigs are highly intelligent animals, very friendly and can be kept as pets, but most people who have the available space will rear pigs for their meat, which is the next stage up in keeping a garden farm and leading a more comprehensively self-sufficient life.

Pig myths Although pigs are often given very bad press and portrayed as being greedy and dirty, this simply isn't the case. True, they get hungry and like to eat, and true, they make pig noises when they eat – but they are, after all, pigs. Pigs will eat anything; they are foragers and rooters, and will clear your land and undergrowth, devour any kitchen or garden surpluses and turn all this into meat for your table. They're also very useful at digging up your vegetable plot at the end of the season and they'll provide your soil with invaluable manure while they're doing it.

BELOW: Mother pig with her litter rootling for worms, acorns and seeds.

Pigs don't smell. If they do, then it's the food they eat that smells. Traditionally, commercial pig farmers would fill giant vats with pig swill – waste food collected from restaurants and households and then boiled up, which resulted in a substance with a pungent smell and hence a pig's reputation for smelling. This practice has now ceased and pigs are fed on commercially produced pig feed.

Preparing for pigs When deciding to embark on keeping pigs for meat, make contact with a local experienced keeper and breeder. It's also well worth enrolling on a pig-keeping course. These are often held over just one day. They will be able to advise you on how to find out about the best breeds and teach you vital animal husbandry

skills that you'll need, as well as putting you in contact with your local abattoir so that you can arrange to have your pigs slaughtered and butchered when the time comes.

Rare breeds, such as the Tamworth or the Gloucester Old Spot, are often popular choices for their superior-quality meat.

Pigs are herd animals and need to be kept with other pigs. Generally, people start off buying a couple of weaners at about eight weeks old and take them through to pork weight at about six months old, then have them slaughtered locally.

Once you've bought your pigs, you'll then need to transport them home enclosed, so a trailer or a horsebox is the best means. It's possible to bring them home in the back of the car in a dog crate, but pigs make an ear-splitting squeal and may also defecate in the back of the car. The quicker you get them home, the better, and don't forget to open all the windows!

Pig-keeping principles One of the major factors to be considered when keeping pigs is space. A happy pig is a free-range pig with plenty of open space and shelter. Electric fencing is the easiest option, being easy to install, portable and efficient at containing the animals. Pigs naturally root, which means that they dig up the earth and in doing so will create mud. You'll need at least 14 sq m (150 sq ft) per pig to keep mud problems from developing, and in wet areas, this figure can treble. Many pig keepers will move pigs around if the ground becomes too muddy.

Pigs need a shelter that protects them from the elements, particularly from the wind and the sun, as they can suffer from wind- and sunburn. Two pigs can be housed in an A-frame hut that can either be specifically bought or made from timber, corrugated iron or straw bales with a corrugated iron roof. Their housing needs to be strong so that the pigs can't trample or eat it, which they'll do whenever they get the chance.

They don't need to be confined to an area in the garden. If you have the land, they will enjoy roaming in woodland, feeding on wild food such as acorns, sweet chestnuts and elderberries.

Pigs must be fed regularly every day and, depending on their ages, several times per day. The most satisfying part of feeding time will be when you delight in them eating up all your kitchen scraps. Keep a 'pig bucket' in a cupboard near the kitchen sink so that you can scrape all the leftovers into it and give to them as part of their diet. You can throw almost everything you eat into the pig bucket, including tea bags, eggshells, milk and eggs, but don't give them meat. Most kitchens won't be able to provide enough waste from scraps alone, so you'll need to supplement their diet with a complete pig mix that can be bought from your animal feed store. They must also have a constant supply of clean, fresh water every day.

Tip: Pigs love to be groomed. A stiff brush or strong fingernails can send a pig into a trance, and also provides an ideal opportunity for you to check your animals over to see if they are in good condition and to enjoy relating to them.

BELOW: Pigs are scrupulously clean – make sure they have clean straw and a dry house to sleep in.

Useful addresses and websites

Nicki Trench's own websites

www.nickitrench.com
www.nickitrench.blogspot.co.uk
For information on vegetable growing and hen keeping.

Societies

Soil Association
South Plaza
Marlborough Street
Bristol
BS1 3NX
Tel: 0117 314 5000
www.soilassociation.org
Promotes planet-friendly food and gardening.

Soil Association Scotland
18C Liberton Brae
Tower Mains
Edinburgh
EH16 6AE
Tel: 0131 666 2474

Royal Horticultural Society
80 Vincent Square
London
SW1P 2PE
Tel: 0845 260 5000
info@rhs.org.uk
www.rhs.org.uk
For general gardening advice.

National Society of Allotment and Leisure Gardeners
O'Dell House
Hunters Road
Corby
Northants
NN17 5JE
Tel: 01536 266576
natsoc@nsalg.org.uk
www.nsalg.org.uk
For information on allotments.

Federation of City Farms and Community Gardens
The Green House
Hereford Street
Bristol
BS3 4NA
Tel: 0117 923 1800
admin@farmgarden.org.uk
www.farmgarden.org.uk
Promotes community-managed farms and gardens across the UK.

Garden Organic
Coventry
Warwickshire
CV8 3LG
Tel: 02476 303517
enquiry@gardenorganic.org.uk
www.gardenorganic.co.uk
The UK's leading organic growing charity is dedicated to researching and promoting organic gardening, farming and food.

National Vegetable Growing Society
Tel: 01382 580394
www.nvsuk.org.uk
Advice on growing and showing vegetables.

The Herb Society
PO Box 946
Northampton
NN3 0BN
Tel: 0845 491 8699
info@herbsociety.org.uk
www.herbsociety.org.uk
Educational charity dedicated to encouraging the appreciation and use of herbs.

Fruit Expert
Daresbury Point
Green Wood Drive
Manor Park
Cheshire
WA7 1UP
janem@fruitexpert.co.uk
www.fruitexpert.co.uk
Features and articles on all kinds of fruit.

British Summer Fruits
10 Rathbone Place
London
W1T 1HP
Tel: 020 7439 2780
www.britishsummerfruits.co.uk
Promotes British-grown soft and stone fruits.

Compassion in World Farming
River Court
Mill Lane
Godalming
Surrey
GU7 1EZ
Tel: 01483 521953
www.ciwf.org.uk
For information on humane and organic methods of farming.

Garden Action
webmaster@gardenaction.co.uk
www.gardenaction.co.uk
For general advice on gardening and growing vegetables.

Recycle Now
Tel: 0845 331 3131
www.recyclenow.com
Find out how and where to recycle.

Meadow Land and Money
Tel: 01403 262523
www.meadowlandmoney.co.uk
Lists plots of land for sale.

National Trust
PO Box 39
Warrington
WA5 7WD
Tel: 0844 800 1895
enquiries@thenationaltrust.org.uk
www.nationaltrust.org.uk
For information on gardening and allotments.

Landshare
info@landshare.net
www.landshare.net
Website connecting landowners with growers.

FARMA
Lower Ground Floor
12 Southgate Street
Winchester
Hampshire
SO23 9EF
Tel: 0845 4588420
www.localfoods.org.uk
Check the website to find your nearest farmers' market.

Grow Your Own magazine
25 Phoenix Court
Hawkins Road
Colchester
Essex
CO2 8JY
Tel: 01206 505979
Subscriptions enquiries: 0844 815 0030
help@growfruitandveg.co.uk
www.growfruitandveg.co.uk

Seed suppliers and nurseries

Thompson & Morgan
Poplar Lane
Ipswich
Suffolk
IP8 3BU
Tel: 0844 2485383
ccare@thompson-morgan.com
www.thompson-morgan.com

Seeds of Italy
A1 Phoenix Ind Est
Rosslyn Cres
Harrow
Middlesex
HA1 2SP
Tel: 0208 427 5020
grow@italianingredients.com
www.seedsofitaly.com

Chiltern Seeds
114 Crowmarsh Battle Barn
Preston Crowmarsh
Wallingford
OX10 6SL
info@chilternseeds.co.uk
www.chilternseeds.co.uk

MAS Seed Specialists
4 Pinhills
Wenhill Heights
Calne
Wiltshire
SN11 0SA
Tel: 01249 819013
shop@meadowmania.co.uk
www.meadowmania.co.uk

The Real Seed Catalogue
PO Box 18
Newport
Near Fishguard
Pembrokeshire
SA65 0AA
Tel: 01239 821107
info@realseeds.co.uk
www.realseeds.co.uk

The Organic Gardening Catalogue
Riverdene Business Park
Molesey Road
Hersham
Surrey
KT12 4RG
Tel: 01932 253666
www.organiccatalogue.com

Harrod Horticultural
Pinbush Road
Lowestoft
Suffolk
NR33 7NL
Tel: 0845 402 5300
www.harrodhorticultural.com

Rocket Gardens
Treverry Farm
Mawgen
Helston
Cornwall
TR12 6BD
Tel: 0845 6033684
queries@rocketgardens.co.uk
www.rocketgardens.co.uk

Shanks Nursery and Plant Centre
Heathfield Road
Burwash Common
Etchingham
East Sussex
TN19 7NB
Tel: 01435 882060
www.shanksnursery.co.uk

Maynards Fruit Farm
Cross Lane
Ticehurst
East Sussex
TN5 7HQ
Tel: 01580 200394
www.maynardsfruit.co.uk

Mantel Farm
Henley Down
Catsfield
Near Battle
East Sussex
TN33 9BN
Tel: 01424 830357
info@mantel-farm.co.uk
www.mantel-farm.co.uk

Coopers Farm Cottage
Stonegate
East Sussex
TN5 7EH
Tel: 01580 200386
jane@coopersfarmstonegate.co.uk
www.coopersfarmstonegate.co.uk

Compost suppliers

West Riding Organics Ltd
Littleborough
Lancashire
Tel: 01706 379944
wroltd@btconnect.com
www.westridingorganics.co.uk
Soil Association accredited composts.

KPS Composting Services Ltd
KPS House
Ham Lane
Scaynes Hill
West Sussex
RH17 7PR
Tel: 01444 831010
sales@kpscomposting.co.uk
www.kpscomposting.co.uk
Soil Association accredited soil improvers.

Fertile Fibre Ltd
info@fertilefibre.co.uk
www.fertilefibre.com/shop
Soil Association accredited coir-based composts.

Wiggly Wigglers
Lower Blakemere Farm
Blakemere
Herefordshire
HR2 9PX
Tel: 01981 500391
wiggly@wigglywigglers.co.uk
www.wigglywigglers.co.uk
Supplier of wormeries and other gardening products.

Gardening supplies

Dobie's
Long Road
Paignton
Devon
TQ4 7SX
Tel: 0844 701 7625
www.dobies.co.uk

Rustic Garden Supplies
Church Farm House
Wellow
Bath
BA2 8QS
Tel: 01225 332233
sales@rusticgarden.co.uk
www.rusticgarden.co.uk
Vintage garden tools.

Wild Planet Products
80 Brattle Wood
Sevenoaks
Kent
TN13 1QT
Tel: 07825 154424
pamper@wildplanetproducts.com
www.wildplanetproducts.com

Caring for animals

British Hen Welfare Trust
Hope Chapel
Ash Manor
Rose Ash
Devon
EX36 4RF
Tel: 01884 860084
info@bhwt.org.uk
www.bhwt.org.uk

Chicken Out! Campaign
c/o Compassion in World Farming
River Court
Mill Lane
Godalming
Surrey
GU7 1EZ
Tel: 01483 521950
chickenout@ciwf.org
www.chickenout.tv

British Poultry Council
5–11 Lavington Street
London
SE1 0NZ
Tel: 0203 544 1342
info@britishpoultry.org.uk
www.britishpoultry.org.uk
For general advice on keeping hens.

Practical Poultry Magazine
Kelsey Publishing Group
Cudham Tithe Barn
Berry's Hill
Cudham
Kent
TN16 3AG
Tel: 01959 543530
pp.info@kelsey.co.uk
www.practicalpoultry.com

The British Beekeepers' Association
The National Beekeeping Centre
National Agricultural Centre
Stoneleigh Park
Warwickshire
CV8 2LG
Tel: 02476 696679
bbka@britishbeekeepers.com
www.bbka.org.uk
For general advice on beekeeping.

British Goat Society
www.allgoats.com
secretary@allgoats.com
For general advice on keeping goats and the different breeds.

British Pig Association
Trumpington Mews
40b High Street
Trumpington
Cambridge
CB2 9LS
Tel: 01223 845100
bpa@britishpigs.org
www.britishpigs.org.uk
For general advice on keeping pigs and the different breeds.

Index

Author's acknowledgements

This has been a hugely satisfying and fulfilling book to write and I'm extremely grateful for all the help, advice, encouragement and enthusiasm from so many garden farmers. As ever, my thanks to my two daughters, Camilla and Maddy, for being so patient whilst I hogged the computer and was late with dinner on so many occasions over the summer when I was writing – it was a good job the food came from my vegetable patch across the garden and not from the supermarket a long drive halfway across town or we may have starved! And also big thanks to them for helping to style some of the shots; they were particularly keen when assisting with the ones where they could eat the produce!

My particular thanks to Malcolm Husselbee who, as an experienced and accomplished allotment holder, gave me endless and invaluable tips and tricks over the phone – only after he'd tended to his vegetables, of course. Malcolm's knowledge and generosity were very humbling and an inspiration to all of us garden farmers. Allotments are full of experienced gardeners and characters only too willing to share their knowledge, and if you manage to find another 'Malcolm' you will be very lucky and your vegetables much more likely to thrive. Vivien Harper is another inspiration, who generously shared her wonderful vegetable garden, compost heap and herbs and patiently allowed us to just turn up and photograph; Holly from Garden's Maid Tidy, who helped enormously to keep my garden under control while I was busy writing; Laurel and Paul Brummer for their generosity and their stunning hybrid hens, Oliver the cockerel and the Speckled Sussexes and not to mention keeping the greenhouse watered and locking my hens away if ever the need arose; Martin and Dodie Pryke for their location and for also being kind and not laughing when I tripped and fell straight into the middle of their vegetable bed, and to India and Jamie for their beautiful hand modelling, expert apple wrapping and wild food foraging; Jane Howard for sharing her expertise and passion for the art of beekeeping; Alice Nadler for some great tips from the US; Richard Maud-Roxby for letting us photograph his stunning orchard and vegetable garden at the last minute when we thought we'd lost the opportunity of ever finding any peas still in season; Rob and Caroline Cowan for some beautiful location shots, pretty goats and irresistible pigs; Paul Webster, expert woodsman, for his excellent knowledge of wild food; Christopher Hart for being the most brilliant 'photographer's assistant' anyone could wish for.

Finally, a huge thank you to Cindy Richards from CICO Books for commissioning me to write my favourite book so far and to Gillian Haslam for being a fantastic guide along the way. Thank you to Jo Richardson for her work on the text and Sally Powell and Christine Wood for the beautiful layouts. Last, but most definitely not least – to David Merewether for taking the most stunning photographs throughout the book with swiftness and ease, and for being such a pleasurable companion on our photography 'road trips'.